MAGICAL POWER OF NAME

MAGICAL POWER OF NAME

Dr. Piyhalli Roy Gupta

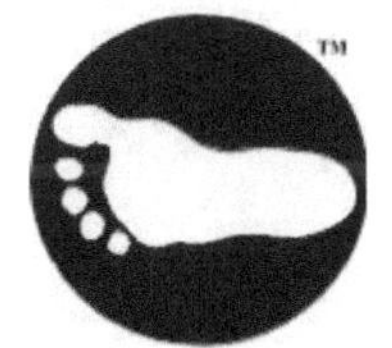

Bigfoot Publications

Because, there's a writer in everyone.

Magical Power Of Name

Author : Dr. Piyhalli Roy Gupta

First Published by

Bigfoot06 Publications (OPC) Pvt. Ltd. B-10,12 Shree Shyam Palace, Sector 4,5 Chowk, Old Railway Road, Gurugram, Haryana (122001)

Website: www.bigfootpublications.in
Email: info@bigfootpublications.com

First Edition : January 2023

© Dr. Piyhalli Roy Gupta

ISBN Print Book - **978-81-960097-6-2**

Printed in India

"Numbers are the thoughts of God."

- St. Augustine

Dedication

*This book is dedicated to my husband Sanjib Roy and my
son Aritra Roy . You are the blessings of my life...*

TABLE OF CONTENTS

PREFACE

Numerology is the wonderful science of Numbers. Though this is an age-old science, its relevance is not less in this modern world. The thirst for knowledge and my inquisitive mind dragged me towards this beautiful subject called Numerology. I am a student of this subject for more than a decade. The reason why I consider myself a student is because of the vastness of this subject; even after learning so much, it still feels like there is so much more to learn.

The way Numerology interprets anyone's life through the date of birth and name is simply unbelievable. This is the secret behind the world-wide popularity of this age-old science called Numerology. Through this book "Magical Power of Name" I would like to make you aware of your power, that lies hidden in your name. I am sure once it is discovered, it may do a miracle for you.

It is said that name is the melody of our soul. So, it is very much important to choose a perfect name either for ourselves or for our business ventures. Name is the doorway through which we can know our Soul purpose. It is this awareness of my soul purpose that always encourages me to spread the knowledge of numbers among other fellow human beings.

The present book "Magical Power of Name" is the result of that awareness. Although I started my career as an English Teacher in a convent school, after a couple of years of working in different schools, I started realizing that something is missing in my life, so I decided to drop my career as a school teacher for good and opened my own Grooming Institute. I was happy with that career but still, I felt a void inside me. Ever since I was introduced to this subject Numerology, I completely understood the reason for my inner void. There was this empty space which had to be filled with the knowledge that this subject gave to me.

This also gave me the reasons as well as a chance to help people with this abundance of knowledge.

In this Journey of writing the book "Magical Power of Name," I owe many people for their support and encouragement which helped me to express my ideas in the format of this book. I feel gratitude to –

Bigfoot Publications for their continuous support and motivation. I strongly believe without their support my manuscript would've never taken the shape of such a beautiful book.

I would like to thank all my gurus who came in my life with their knowledge in various subjects like Numerology, Vastu, Astrology, Palmistry, Tarot card Reading, Oracle card reading, Graphology, NLP, Reiki Healing, Pranic Healing. It's their blessings that inspired me to write this book.

Thanks to all my clients who believed that Numerology can help them to solve their problems and gave me the chance to work for them, without those clients I would've never got a chance to understand all that theoretical knowledge of numbers practically.

Thanks to all my students who respect me as their mentor and always inspire me to achieve more.

Above all, I am grateful to my parents for their support and blessings.

Dr. Piyhalli Roy Gupta

Mob: 9903223629

Website: www.piyhalliroygupta.com

E-Mail – info@piyhalliroygupta.com

INTRODUCTION

"There are many useful and beautiful things human beings can design. But the greatest form of design is if you become the designer of your own Life"

- Sadguru

Modern-day human lives are full of challenges. Every single day, people go through so many things that lead to stress, anxiety, low self-esteem, and lack of confidence. That doesn't only affect the individual but also acts as a reason for destruction in the family. Being overwhelmed by all those challenges, we start looking for solutions outside, but the futile attempt at getting solutions outside makes us all the more puzzled over our life's issues. According to the Lotus sutra "Living beings enjoy themselves at ease". This means we are born to experience joy in our Life. Ignorance of our own self is the key reason behind our lifelong sorrow. That's the reason why it is said "know thyself, then thou shalt know the universe and God". Here lies the greatness of the amazing number science called Numerology, which by the interpretation of numbers coming from our Date of Birth and Name, helps us to understand our true selves and our surroundings as well. It is said that whatever is written in your destiny is surely going to happen, but it is also true that you can change your destiny and make things better by making little changes in your life. Thus, Numerology helps us to become mature and to accept our life challenges. The journey towards success starts with this acceptance.

Your picking up this book clearly indicates that you have a keen desire to understand yourself. Surprisingly your name is the key to understand your true personality. As an author, it is my duty to give you quality information regarding this. We see so many people living their lives but don't have any proper guidance. Even though they have skills and abilities, they are still not able to figure out the reasons for their failure. The result is a complete disappointment and heart breaks. Unknowingly, they make some wrong decisions in their personal life and professional life that make things more miserable. If you feel that something like this is also happening to you or you feel like this is your story only, then I must tell you that this book could be the best companion or guidance of your life. First of all, I would like to congratulate you on making the right decision and choosing this book to read. Many many congratulations once again on joining this group of happy people who have made their lives better with the knowledge of this beautiful subject called Numerology.

So, the time has come when you should stop acting like a victim and take charge of your Life with the power of your name. If you want to create magic with your life then your name is that magic wand. Many years ago I also created that magic in my life with the help of my Numerologically corrected Name Piyhalli (no legal change done). Though the spelling looks a little bit odd but the true fact is that Piyhalli created magic in my life by giving me more self-confidence, undaunted courage, never give up spirit and above all attitude for winning. So, name change means the change of a whole lot of energy in our life.

In my first book "Magical power of Numbers", I have already discussed the importance of Fate Numbers which come from our date of birth. In the present book, I am going to provide you step-by-step guidance to understand the meaning of your name. So, the power is within your name. The knowledge of that power can make a huge difference in your life. I am sure this book will definitely add some value to your present life. It is very important to set the right intention before you start to read this book. Your intention should be to make improvements in your life with the knowledge of this book. Then only the reading of this book will be worth some. Don't treat this book as time pass only rather study seriously, you will get valuable information.

You are about to begin an exciting Journey in your Life.

Wish you all the Best!!

1

NUMEROLOGY AND ITS EVOLUTION

What Is Numerology -

When Mathematics got married to Metaphysics it gave birth to a beautiful subject called Numerology. In simple words, Numerology is the science of Numbers. But the main concern of Numerology is the qualitative value of numbers rather than the quantitative value of numbers. Numerology is such an insightful as well as an extraordinary tool that reveals our destiny's blueprint with the help of our date of birth and name. Among all the branches of Metaphysical Studies, Numerology is the most authentic, easiest, and trustworthy modality for future guidance. Because of its accuracy and flawless guidance, Numerology got worldwide acceptance and popularity among its readers.

Numerology is an age-old science. But this age-old science came to light out of darkness or in other words we can say became modernized by the famous Greek mathematician and mystic Pythagoras who was born in the 6th century BCE. The system that Pythagoras followed became popular as Pythagorean Numerology. In this book "Magical Power of Name" the same Pythagorean system has been followed, as I am an ardent follower and life- long student of Pythagorean Numerology. Pythagoras was the first to declare that the world is made up of numbers. Numerology is not only a brunch of occult science but it is closely related to science, especially physics. In Physics, we have learned that everything that exists has definite motion, in the world of vibratory frequency. Everything in nature has its own rate of vibration. Vibrations are measured only through numbers. That is why numbers are the key to all mysteries because they reveal the vibrational content of all things. That's why we can say that Numerology is based on Physics.

Numerology should not be used only as a tool for future telling. Basically, a man's fortune depends on his thought process and actions which actually come from his own belief system. He can choose to live either in harmony or in disharmony with his life. It is purely up to our free will whether we become the 'victim of fate' or the 'children of destiny'. We are the creator of our own destiny. You might ask then what is the function of Numerology. Numerology can give correct character analysis by analysing your name and date of birth. Numerology can identify the strong qualities of your character as well as shortcomings of your character. Success depends on how will you capitalize on those strong qualities to create opportunities in your life and work on your shortcomings for the upliftment of your soul.

2

<u>NAME (FROM NUMEROLOGICAL ASPECT)</u>

Name is the most important part of anyone's Numerological Chart. Your name is the main essence of who you are. Your name will determine many life experiences that you are going to encounter in this lifetime. Name gives the very first impression of any person. Generally, we love our own name but this is not true for all because there are many who are not comfortable with their own names. The secret behind this is that our names carry energy. Now if you are confused to read this point, let me clear your confusion first. Our name is a combination of a few letters. In Numerology every letter is assigned with a number that has not only its quantitative value but has its own qualitative value. Again, a number has its own frequency vibration. In this way our name carries energy. In another way we can say our name is nothing but sound vibration, the human body is affected by any type of sound vibration. Now imagine if our body gets affected by the positive sound vibration from our name it always gives positive results but, in any case, if it is affected by negative sound vibration it always gives a negative result. A positive result can be felt in the form of good health, mental peace, and happiness. A negative result can be felt in the form of unhappiness, worry, lack of confidence, and confusion in anyone's life. I hope now this is clearly understood how much a name is important in anyone's life. It should be always remembered that the vibration of the given name should not clash with the numbers that come from the date of birth. For example, if anyone has a date of birth of 8/06/1988, then for this person 8 name number can bring serious negative consequences.

<u>Choosing The Child's Name</u> –

Parenting a child is no doubt a great task in anyone's life. It is the duty of parents to ensure a healthy environment for their child so that the hidden talent in the child may come out. So, the first task for parents is to discover the hidden talent in their child, then only parents can give proper guidance to their child. When the child is born, the first thing parents need to do is to give him or her a name by which people will address him or her. That name is not only the identity of the child but also holds the complete future of the child. So, it is the duty of parents that, while choosing the name for their child, they should take the help of Numerology. Because correct name vibration helps to shape up one's career as well.

So, what we can understand from this is that while giving a name to the newborn parents should not go with their emotional point of view. Choosing a name that carries positive vibration is the first gift that they can give to the child which will help the child to do well in his studies and flourish in his career in the long run. Parents should try to give such name to their child that create a feel-good factor because I have seen many clients complaining that they don't feel good about their names since their childhood days. So, while choosing the name parents are advised to listen to their intuition because spiritually it is believed that parents especially the mother gets the intuition to choose the name for the child. So, the mother's preference must be given priority, when choosing the name for the newborn. Hence while selecting the name for the newborn don't go by emotion only pay attention to your intuition.

One more piece of advice parents should follow is not to call their child by too many names. As each name carries energy, so too many names mean too much energy which brings confusion in a child's life. Numerologically it is recommended that stick to one or two names only for your child, don't mess up your child's life by using different names.

<u>Choosing Company Name</u> –

In the business world as well, name is very much important. People spend a lot in selecting a good name for their company and brand. The reason is the same so that the positive vibration of the name brings success to their venture. That is why in the business world name is equivalent to money. We have seen that after putting in all the efforts many companies do not run well and have to see lots of losses. Remember a Numerologically compatible business name for a company helps to sustain the competition in the business world. The company name vibration should always be compatible with the vibration of the owner. In the case of a partnership company, the company name vibration should be compatible with the vibrations of all the partners. The company name vibration also should be compatible with the kinds of service it provides. For example, 2 company name vibration is good for food, customer service provider business. 4 company name vibration is good for architecture, and construction-oriented businesses. 5 company name vibration is good for media-related business. 11/2 company name is good for the film industry. Remember if anything in this world has a name, it has a number as well be it a movie, serial, website, book title, or any product. So before starting any new business venture, give positive vibration to your business by selecting a lucky business name.

3

METAPHYSICAL MEANING OF NUMBERS

1

(Original – Independent – Aggressive)

1 is the most unconventional of all numbers. 1 represents male characteristics. 1 is full of courage and creative energy. 1 represents leadership and high ambition. 1 is goal oriented and self-reliant. 1 indicates any sort of beginning. Negative 1 represents arrogance, selfishness, limitation, ego, stubbornness, strongly opinionated and low self-esteem.

CORRESPONDENTS

Planet – The Sun

Letters – A, J, S

Element – Fire

Astrological House – Aries

Tarot – The Magician

Numbers – 10, 19, 28, 37, 46, 55, 64, 73, 82, 91, 100

Day – Sunday

Months – January and October

Birthdays – 1, 10, 19, 28

Gemstone – Ruby or Garnet

Colour – Red

Musical Notes – C and C #

Friendly Numbers – 1, 2, 3, 4, 7, 9

Neutral Numbers – 5

Enemy Numbers – 6, 8

2

(Peace maker – Adaptable – Gentle)

2 is the gentlest of all numbers. 2 is feminine, and very much cooperative. 2 is very much emotional as well. It always likes harmonious situations and dislikes any sort of confrontation. 2 is a very much friendly number. Negative 2 is uncooperative, lacks self-confidence, and is over-sensitive, very much depressive and melancholic in nature.

CORRESPONDENTS

Planet – The Moon

Letters – B, K, T

Element – Water

Astrological House – Taurus

Tarot – The High Priestess

Numbers – 11, 20, 29, 38, 47, 56, 65, 74, 83, 92, 101

Day – Monday

Months – February, November

Birthdays – 2, 11, 20, 29

Gemstone – Moonstone

Colour – Orange

Musical Notes – D and D #

Friendly Numbers – 1, 2, 4, 5, 7

Neutral Numbers – 3, 6, 8, 9

3

(Creative, Sociable, Communicative)

3 is the combination of 1 male energy and 2 female energy. 3 is full of artistic and musical talent. 3 has an inherent quality of self-expression. 3 is a very much friendly and happy-go-lucky type of number. 3 always represents the mind, body, and soul connection. 3 is joyful, charismatic, extrovert, and has a good sense of humour. The negative 3 is very much talkative, scattered, boastful, very Indiscipline, disorganized, moody, and cynical. Negative 3 sometimes suffers from an inferiority complex. Negative 3 is unforgiving, introvert, leaves, things unfinished.

<u>CORRESPONDENTS</u>

Planet – Jupiter

Letters – C, L, U

Element – Air

Astrological House – Gemini

Tarot – The Empress

Numbers – 12, 21, 30, 39, 48, 57, 66, 75, 84, 93, 102

Day – Thursday

Months – March, December

Birthdays – 3, 12, 21, 30

Gemstone – Topaz

Colour – Yellow

Musical Notes – E and F

Friendly Numbers – 1, 2, 3, 4, 7, 9

Neutral Numbers – 8

Enemy Numbers – 5, 6

4

(Practical, discipline, stable)

4 is the most practical of all numbers. It is very much reliable. 4 is synonymous with system and order. 4 is a very protective number. 4 is down to earth in nature. 3 ds matching with 4, they are dependable, disciplined, and determined. Negative 4 is very much rigid and dislikes any type of change. It is workaholic, insensitive. Negative 4 procrastinates things and is full of prejudices.

CORRESPONDENTS

Planet – The Earth

Letters – D, M, V

Element – Earth

Astrological House – Cancer

Tarot – The Emperor

Numbers – 13, 22, 31, 40, 49, 58, 67, 76, 85, 94, 103

Day – Sunday

Month – April

Birthdays – 4, 13, 22, 31

Gemstone – Emerald, Green Jade

Colour – Green

Musical Notes – F#

Friendly Numbers – 1, 2, 4, 7

Neutral Numbers – 3, 5, 9

Enemy Numbers – 6, 8

5

(Active, versatile, adventurous)

5 is the most dynamic of all numbers. 5 is a freedom lover, and 5 is a very much dynamic number. 5 can juggle many works at the same time. 5 loves to travel. 5 is also called the number of travellers. 5 can't settle in one place. 5 is very much witty. 5 can make friends very easily. 5 loves to enjoy life. 5 loves sexual pleasure. Negative 5 is very much addictive, irresponsible, lacks consistency, and impulsive in nature.

<u>CORRESPONDENTS</u>

Planet – Mercury

Letters –E, N, W

Element – Fire

Astrological House – Leo

Tarot – The Hierophant

Numbers – 14, 23, 32, 41, 50, 59, 68, 77, 86, 95, 104

Day – Wednesday

Month – May

Birthdays – 5, 14, 23

Gemstone – Turquoise

Colour – Turquoise

Musical Notes – G and G#

Friendly Numbers – 1, 4, 6

Neutral Numbers – 3, 6, 8, 9

Enemy Numbers – 2, 7

6

(Responsible, compassionate, healer)

6 is the most loving of all numbers. 6 represents love for family, peace, and harmony. 6 is a number of balance, love, and compassion. 6 is loyal, peaceful, and religious in nature. 6 is born teacher. 6 is a very caring number, especially for those who are weak in society. 6 is a creative number but when becomes negative it expresses tension and anxiety. Negative 6 is a possessive, jealous, perfectionist.

<u>CORRESPONDENTS</u>

Planet – Venus

Letters – F, O, X

Elements – Earth and Water

Astrological House – Virgo

Tarot – The Lovers

Numbers – 15, 24, 33, 42, 51, 60, 69, 78, 87, 96, 105

Day – Friday

Month – June

Birthdays – 6, 15, 24

Gemstones – Diamond, Blue, Sapphire, Blue- white pearl

Colour – Blue

Musical Notes – A and A#

Friendly Numbers – 5, 6, 8, 9

Neutral Numbers – 2, 3, 4, 7

Enemy Numbers – 1

7

(Intuitive, Introspective, Philosophical)

7 is a temple number, very much spiritual in nature. 7 likes solitude, and always avoids the hustle and bustle of life. 7 is withdrawn in nature. 7 loves to contemplate and meditate.7 is very much trustworthy. It prefers old things, especially things that are antique in nature.7 loves to accumulate knowledge and wisdom. Negative 7 is addictive, spiritual, and aloof. Negative 7 is unfaithful, dishonest, cruel, try to control things.

CORRESPONDENTS

Planet – Neptune

Letters – G, P, Y

Element – Water

Astrological House – Libra

Tarot – The chariot

Numbers – 16, 25, 34, 43, 52, 61, 70, 79, 88, 97, 106

Days – Sunday, Monday

Month – July

Birthdays – 7, 16, 25

Gemstone – Amethyst

Colour – Violet

Musical Notes – B

Friendly Numbers – 1, 2, 4, 5, 7

Neutral Numbers – 3, 6, 8, 9

8

(Good Judgement, Power, Recognition)

8 is the most result oriented of all numbers. 8 represents the balance between the material and spiritual world. 8 is powerful, ambitious, and money conscious. 8 is a very much business number. 8 can undertake big ventures. 8 is also a number of visionaries. The negative 8 has poor money management skills. It is selfish, self-centred, has little faith in self, always blames others, lacks perseverance, mentally indolent, and misses opportunities. As a result, meets with constant failure.

CORRESPONDENTS

Planet – Saturn

Letters – H, Q, Z

Element – Earth

Astrological House – Scorpio

Tarot – Strength

Numbers – 17, 26, 35, 44, 53, 62, 71, 80, 89, 98, 107

Day – Saturday

Months – August

Birthdays – 8, 17, 26

Gemstone – Diamond

Colour – Gray

Musical Notes – High C

Friendly Numbers – 5, 6

Neutral Numbers – 3

Enemy Numbers – 1, 2, 4, 7, 9

9

(Compassion, tolerance, self-less service)

9 is the most humanitarian of all numbers. It is the number of giving, sharing, and loving. 9 is broad-minded. 9 expresses idealism and unconditional love for others. 9 is intuitive and has a strong desire to help mankind. 9 has artistic expression and is a wise counsellor. Negative 9 has emotional imbalance and lacks compassion. It can't let go of things very easily and demands recognition.

CORRESPONDENTS

Planet – Mars

Letters – I, R

Element – Fire

Astrological House – Sagittarius

Tarot – The Hermit

Numbers – 18, 27, 36, 45, 54, 63, 72, 81, 90, 99, 108

Day – Monday

Month – September

Birthdays – 9, 18, 27

Gemstone – Opal

Colour – Saffron

Musical Notes – High D

Friendly Numbers – 1, 2, 3, 4, 7, 9

Neutral Numbers – 6, 8

Enemy Numbers – 5

4

<u>MASTER NUMBERS</u>

There are a few double-digit numbers in Numerology, which are called Master Numbers. Master Numbers possess more power than other Numbers. But as they are very much powerful numbers so they are sometimes difficult to handle. Our body- mind-soul are highly impacted when we carry this number either in our date of birth or in our Name. The most important Master Numbers are 11 and 22. 11 is the higher vibration of 2 and 22 is the higher vibration of 4.

<u>Master Number 11</u>

(Intuitive, Visionary, Spiritual)

11 is a number of visionary and full of psychic abilities. 11 has all the qualities of 2 but in a more intense manner. 11 is very much charismatic and highly inspirational in nature. 11 is the most intuitive of all the numbers in Numerology. Number 11 has high spiritual vibration; it gives a higher level of consciousness. 11 has excellent voice power which can attract people through verbal skill either through speaking or singing. That's why many spiritual gurus and singers have 11 in their Numerology chart. Negative 11 is very much dangerous, it can go up to self-destruction. Negative 11 is shy, timid, non–communicative, narrow-minded, and above all lacks self-confidence.

Master Number 22

(Master Builder, Great organizer, Mystic)

22 is the most powerful of all Numbers. It is called the Number of Master Builders. 22 is very much diplomatic and highly intelligent. 22 has all the potential for a big dream to manifest. It has big ideas and great plans. It must work towards the realization of bigger goals. It has the combination of the spirituality of the number 11 and the practicality of 4 (2+2=4). 22 is a highly ambitious number. Negative 22 lacks energy, lacks organizing power, and can't keep a commitment.

5

KARMIC DEBT NUMBERS

As a part of Metaphysical Science, Numerology is based on Soul Theory. According to this theory, our soul had incarnated many times before this lifetime. Every time it incarnated it created karma both positive and negative, which is quite normal. In Numerology Karmic Debt Numbers are the indications of Karma baggage that we have been carrying from our previous lifetime. There are total four Karmic Debt Numbers in Numerology. They are 13, 14, 16, and 19. When these karmic Debt Numbers appear in our Numerology Birth Chart, they give us some special lessons. Though the learning process of these lessons are tough if we can learn them properly, our soul gets a chance to evolve in the process.

KARMIC DEBT NUMBER -13

13 Karmic Debt Number always gives us obstacles in our way to fulfill our dream. Those who carry this number either in their Date of Birth or in their Name have to do a lot of hard work to become successful. For them, patience is the main key to get success. Many with 13 Karmic Debt Number fall into the trap of laziness which brings failure in their Lives. So those who have a 13 Karmic Debt Number must remember not to apply any short cut in fulfilling their dreams.

You can bypass the negative effects of Karmic Debts by praying, giving, and asking for forgiveness. If it comes in your Name through Expression

Number, Soul Urge Number, or Personality Number you can correct the Name spelling to ease your sufferings.

KARMIC DEBT NUMBER - 14

14 Karmic Debt Number appears in the Numerology Birth Chart when you misuse personal freedom, especially in the case of sexual pleasure in past lives. Those who carry this number either in Date of Birth or in Name can easily become prey to all kinds of addiction like drugs, alcohol, food, and sex. Temptation comes into life very easily. So, one needs to exercise self-control in every aspect of life, if this Karmic Debt Number appears in the Birth Chart. This karmic Debt Number actually gives you lessons in self-control and commitment. You need to avoid all kinds of sensory pleasure. Setting a worthy goal is very much important to maintain discipline in life. The appearance of this karmic Debt Number in the Numerology Birth Chart may also indicate accidents, sickness, or even property loss, or failure in business. This Karmic Debt Number makes life out of balance. You start procrastinating things. In case you have a 14 Karmic Debt Number you need to understand the proper meaning of personal freedom.

You can bypass the negative effects of Karmic Debts by praying, giving, and asking for forgiveness. If it comes in your Name through Expression Number, Soul Urge Number, or Personality Number you can correct the Name spelling to ease your sufferings.

KARMIC DEBT NUMBER - 16

16 Karmic Debt number always gives us ego-related problems. 16 Karmic Debt Number means conflict between the higher self and the lower self, where the defeat of the lower self is sure. The process is quite painful. It is a number of rebirths. 16 Karmic Debt Number gives us the lesson of Faith and Gratitude without Faith your aspiration never comes to a realization. When 16 Karmic Debt Number appears in the Numerology Birth chart, there always may be a chance of failure when you come near to your Goal. But by the power of faith, you overcome your failure and start once again. You will get God's guidance if you

believe in Him. You need to maintain a positive attitude toward your life. You can get all your answers in your silence and meditation. With an understanding of the proper meaning of spiritualism, you can shade your false ego. With your service attitude to humanity, you can create new paradigms in your life.

You can bypass the negative effects of Karmic Debts by praying, giving, and asking for forgiveness. If it comes in your Name through Expression Number, Soul Urge Number, or Personality Number you can correct the Name spelling to ease your sufferings.

<u>KARMIC DEBT NUMBER -19</u>

19 Karmic Debt Number gives us difficulties in all aspects of life. Actually, these difficulties are a boon in disguise because if the 19 Karmic Debt Number appears in our Numerology Birth Chart either in Date of Birth or in Name, it means we need to learn the lesson of self-dependence. But this process of learning independence is painful. These Karmic Debt Numbers make us loners. So, we should serve our community in such a way that makes us connected with others. Those who have this Karmic Debt Number have to suffer the first twenty years mentally, physically, and emotionally, but in these sufferings, they get trained to become a potential leader in their respective fields.

You can bypass the negative effects of Karmic Debts by praying, giving, and asking for forgiveness. If it comes in your Name through Expression Number, Soul Urge Number, or Personality Number you can correct the Name spelling to ease your sufferings.

6

METAPHYSICAL MEANING OF LETTER A TO Z

Every letter in English Alphabet has its own meaning with its positive and negative sides. Once we have knowledge of this, we can understand anything from any given name. Numerology interprets each letter of the English Alphabet in a different way. Numerology connects every letter with a number. Every number is connected with one planet and carrying all the features of that particular planet. In the earlier chapter, we have already discussed it. In this way, every English letter has its own quantitative value as well as qualitative value. As per nature, all these English letters are divided into four categories Mental, Physical, Emotional, and Intuitive. In Future Prediction through Numerology letters play an important role. While interpreting any name, the first letter and the first vowel of the name have their own effects on our character. The missing letters in our name are also an indicator of the lessons that we must learn in this lifetime. Each letter in our name has its own contribution to create different events in our life. Each letter has a specific time duration for its influence.

(Independent, Ambitions, Creative)

A as the 1st letter of the English Alphabet carries with it all the attributes of the Number 1. A comes under the category of a Mental Letter. The shape of the capital letter A shows firmness. A shows balance and self-control. The bar in the center indicates self-importance. A is ambitious, active, original, and very good planner. A is very much creative. Negative A shows a lot of ego and likes to start things but not finish them.

In Future Prediction through Numerology A indicates travel, residential change, promotion, and opportunities.

B

(Gentle, Diplomatic, Friendly)

B as the 2nd letter of the English Alphabet carries with it all the attributes of the Number 2. B comes under the category of an Emotional Letter. If we look at the shape of B, we can see two circles connected to a vertical line. The top circle indicates the spiritual side and the bottom circle indicates the material side. B is the collector of occult knowledge. B is very much loyal to friends. B is very much intuitive. B falls in love very easily. Negative B is moody, dishonest, secretive, and melancholic.

In Future predication through Numerology B indicates deep emotional love affairs, and health problems especially nervous related.

C

(Sociable, Intuitive, Optimistic)

C as the 3rd letter of the English Alphabet carries with it all the attributes of the number 3. C comes under the category of Intuitive Letter. If we look at the shape of C, it is a half-circle. C is Open minded, loves to talk. C has psychic abilities. C is very much optimistic. C has artistic talent. C has good speaking power. The intellectual property of C is very high. Negative C scatters its talent, lacks self–expression, and worries over little things. Negative C can't handle money properly.

In Future Prediction through Numerology C indicates a good time for business and different social gatherings.

D

(Practical, Honest, Stubborn)

D as the 4th letter of the English Alphabet carries with it all the attributes of the Number 4. D comes under the category of a Physical Letter. If we look at the shape of the Letter D, we can see that it is a closed letter which indicates limitations and restrictions. D is a nature lover, loyal and honest. D is reliable, family-oriented, and good at completing any project. Negative D is very much rigid, serious, and workaholic. Negative D is argumentative and very much indecisive. D must learn to see the higher side of life and learn to be optimistic.

In Future Prediction through Numerology D indicates travel, and opportunity for growth. It also indicates some sort of health problems and not a good time for a love relationship.

(Freedom lover, Intuitive, Restless)

E as the 5th letter of the English Alphabet carries with it all the attributes of the Number 5. E comes under the category of Physical Letter. If we look at the shape of the Letter E, we can see that three prongs are pointing to the right always, expecting some sort of change or new experience. The straight line with which the three prongs are attached indicates spiritual interest. E is very social, entertaining, and fond of dresses. E is romantic in nature. E loves to study occult subjects. Negative E is very much sensual and interested in physical things rather than spiritual things. Negative E is deceitful, irresponsible, and liar.

In Future Prediction through numerology E indicates a change of residence, travel, new love affairs, and good financial opportunities.

(Stable, Responsible, Dislikes Criticism)

F as the 6th letter of the English Alphabet carries with it all the attributes of the number 6. F comes under the category of Intuitive Letter. If we look at the shape of the Letter F, we can see that two prongs are pointing to the right always extending helping hands to others. F is very much idealist, intellectual, and purposeful. F has musical talent and artistic ability as well. F loves to serve others. Negative F takes too many responsibilities which creates stress on them. Negative F is abusive, doubtful, and exaggerates things unnecessarily.

In Future Prediction through Numerology F indicates domestic responsibility, a good time for some sort of spiritual growth.

G

(Imaginative, Patient, Lacks Confidence)

G as the 7th letter of the English Alphabet carries with it all the attributes of the number 7. G comes under the category of Mental Letter. If we look at the shape of the letter G, we can resemble the letter with the hump and neck of the camel. The shape of the letter G indicates its introspective nature. G has a very good spiritual understanding, very analytical, doesn't like crowd, and likes to work alone. G possesses a great deal of wisdom. G loves to do things in a bigger way. G loves music. Negative G is secretive, sarcastic, shy, aloof, deceptive, difficult to understand, critical of others, and uses hateful words.

In Future Prediction through Numerology G indicates some sort of financial gain.

(Powerful, Methodical, Escapist)

H as the 8th letter of the English Alphabet carries with it all the attributes of the number 8. H comes under the category of Mental Letter. If we look at the shape of the letter H, we find two straight lines, connected with a bar, which gives similarity with a ladder. The upper half of the letter H indicates the spiritual world, and the lower half indicates the material world. Both feet firmly on the ground indicate great success in the materialistic world. H is a good organizer, logical, and a very good planner. H has good reasoning abilities. H loves music and art. H has good concentration power and a well-balanced attitude towards life. Negative H is judgmental, demanding, fearful, selfish, and miser.

In Future Prediction through Numerology H indicates either monetary gain or loss. deep emotional issues may happen this time.

I

(Artistic, Humanitarian, Emotional)

I as the 9th letter of the English Alphabet carries with it all the attributes of the number 9. I comes under the category of an Emotional Letter. If we look at the shape of the letter I, we can see a vertical line, which indicates great spiritual understanding. I is very much humanitarian at heart and shows a lot of love for others. I thinks a lot about the upliftment of society. I is extremely intellectual, very original, and has literary or artistic abilities. I loves to read books. Negative I is self-centered, egocentric, always thinks about their own interest, impatient, extremely nervous, and forgetful.

In Future Prediction through Numerology, I indicates an opportunity for success and financial benefit. But sometimes it also indicates delays or accidents.

J

(Optimistic, Innovative, Lazy)

J is the first double-digit number (10) in the English Alphabet which is the higher value of 1. Pythagoras assigned the number 1 to this letter J. J carries all the attributes of a number 1. J comes under the category of Mental Letter. If we look at the shape of the letter J, we can see its tail facing left, which means J always refers to past experience. J possesses a very sharp memory. J is very much ambitious and loves to give self-importance. J is very witty and religious at heart. J is very much self-dependent. Negative J suffers from lack of self-confidence and sometimes serious mental tensions. Negative J is hesitant and procrastinates a lot.

In Future Prediction through Numerology J indicates career change or emotional trouble at the beginning but reward after the struggle.

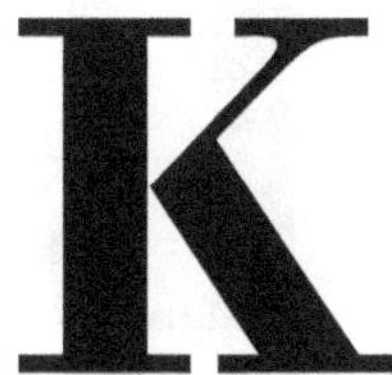

(Friendly, Adventurous, Disconnected)

K is the 11th letter of the English Alphabet. 11 is known as a Master Number in Numerology. 11 is the higher value of the number 2. So, K carries all the attributes of master number 11 and as well as 2. K comes under the category of Intuitive Letter. If we look at the shape of the letter K, we can see it has one straight line with two forks going up and down. It gives the ability to grab the opportunity. In the letter K there are two 'v 's where upper v gives spiritual inclination and lower v gives material inclination. Balance is very important for K to get Spiritual Enlightenment. K always shows extremes either in a positive sense or a negative sense. If it is happy then it is extremely happy if it is unhappy then it is extremely sad. Negative k is too much emotional, dishonest and intolerant.

In Future Prediction through Numerology K indicates nervous tension and new business opportunity.

(Charitable, Balanced, Sensual)

L is the 12th letter of the English Alphabet. Pythagoras assigned the number 3 (1+2=3) to the letter L. So, L carries all the attributes of the number 3. L comes under the category of a Mental Letter. If we look at the shape of the letter L, we can see it has a firm baseline which indicates its focus towards any work. Unlike C it never scatters its energy. L is very creative. L has an interest in occult studies. Unlike C, L retains whatever it gathers. L is philanthropic in nature. L is very much popular in the group, L leads an active life, sociable and friendly in nature. Negative L is too much emotional, suffers from frustration and indecisiveness, and is impatient.

In Future Prediction through Numerology L gives travel and marriage.

M

(Courageous, Reliable, Workaholic)

M is the 13th letter of the English Alphabet. 13 is the Karmic Number in Numerology. Pythagoras assigned the number 4 (1+3= 4) to the letter M. So, M carries all the attributes of the number 4. M comes under the category of a Physical Letter. If we look at the shape of the letter M, we can see there is a v shape in the middle of the letter which gives open-mindedness towards higher thought. M has a very sharp memory. It is creative and productive. M has originality as well as spirituality. Negative M is very much rigid, temperamental, and careless.

In Future Prediction through Numerology M indicates unhappy love affairs and demanding relationships.

(Adaptable, Sensual, Risk Taker)

N is the 14th letter of the English Alphabet. 14 is the Karmic Number in Numerology. Pythagoras assigned the number 5 (1+4=5) to the letter N. So, N carries all the attributes of the number 5. N comes under the category of a Mental Letter. If we look at the shape of the letter N, we can see two 'v's make the letter N. one upside down and the other upright. N is very adaptable to any situation. N is a clear thinker, wins arguments with reason and logic. N always wants to do daring things and loves to take risky chances. N has a spiritual inclination. Negative N suffers from lots of fluctuations in life. Negative N is argumentative, stubborn, highly emotional, and wants to gratify sensual desire.

In Future Prediction through Numerology N indicates a change of residence and brings sensual matters to life.

(Disciplined, Spiritual, Judgmental)

O is the 15th letter of the English Alphabet. Pythagoras assigned the number 6 (1+5=6) to this letter O. So, O carries all the attributes of 6. O comes under the category of an Emotional Letter. If we look at the shape of the letter O, we can see that O is a full circle, which means O is very protective. As a closed letter, it signifies that O holds emotions inside. O can maintain a balance between personal and professional life very successfully. O loves all sorts of beautiful things. O is very much loving, and caring and shows responsibility towards family, friends, and needy people. It has great imaginative power. Negative O is moody, impulsive, jealous, suspicious, cynical, and possessive.

In Future Prediction through Numerology O gives temptation, black magic, and trouble.

P

(Influential, Knowledgeable, Shrewd)

P is the 16th letter of the English Alphabet. 16 is the karmic Number in Numerology. Pythagoras assigned the number 7 (1+6=7) to this letter. So, P carries all the attributes of the number 7. P comes under the category of a Mental Letter. P has excellent power of writing as well as speaking. If we look at the shape of the letter, we can see a circle at the top of the line which represents the human head, which actually represents the pituitary gland. When this pituitary gland becomes active it gives intuitive power, and psychic abilities. P has the wisdom that comes from a higher plane. P has the intellectual capacity, expressed through literary or artistic pursuit. As an enclosed letter P hides its feelings very easily from others. P likes to remain alone, never comfortable in crowed. P likes to maintain its individuality, and this nature brings uniqueness to P. Negative P is stubborn, opinionated, argumentative, moody, deceptive intolerant, tactless, and not a good marriage or business partner.

In Future Prediction through Numerology P brings secret love affairs, accidents, defects, and danger.

(Energetic, stable, Greedy)

Q is the 17th letter of the English Alphabet. Pythagoras assigned the number 8 (1+7=8) to this letter Q. So, Q carries all the attributes of the number 8. Q comes under the category of an Intuitive Letter. Q always looks for new opportunities. Q is determined with strong willpower. Physically and mentally Q is very much active. Q wants harmony and comfort at home. Q is charming, loyal, sympathetic, and dependable. Q has a greater aspiration towards leadership. Negative Q is demanding, greedy, and very much materialistic.

In Future Prediction through Numerology Q indicates the time for financial growth.

R

(Harmonious, Peacemaker, Confused)

R is the 18th letter of the English Alphabet. Pythagoras assigned the number 9 (1+8=9) to this letter R. So, R carries all the attributes of 9, along with some of the attributes of 1 and 8 as well. R comes under the category of an Emotional Letter. R is the most selfless and understanding letter of the English Alphabet. R shows great tolerance to others. R likes to investigate strange events. R is very much psychic and intuitive. R shows brotherhood and unconditional love towards others.

Negative R gets into trouble with the law. R is jealous lustful and greedy. R is very much rude to others, lustful and greedy.

In Future Prediction through Numerology R indicates personal growth, sickness, delay, and accidents.

S

(Magnetic, Energetic, Impulsive)

S is the 19th letter of the English Alphabet. 19 is the karmic Number in Numerology. Pythagoras assigned the number 1 (1+9=10=1) to the letter S. So, S carries all the attributes of 1 and some of the attributes of 9 as well. S comes under the category of an Emotional Letter. S is very much goal oriented. S has leadership skills and prefers to work alone. S has a lot of positivity. S possesses great wisdom and is very much spiritual in nature. Negative S is very depressed, and can't take orders from anyone.

In Future Prediction through Numerology S indicates some sort of new beginning and extreme emotion.

T

(Cooperative, Restless, Over Emotional)

T is the 20th letter of the English Alphabet. Pythagoras assigned the number 2 (2+0=2) to this letter T. So, T carries all the attributes of the number 2. T comes under the category of an Emotional Letter. If we look at the shape of the letter T we can see a perpendicular line and a bar at the top, which indicates the spiritual character of T. T is very much helpful, charming, and like to collect things. Travel is very much important for T. T shows righteousness in his attitude. T gets easily hurt and expects a lot from others. Negative T is stubborn, can't take decisions easily, and is sarcastic.

In Future Prediction through Numerology T indicates something new to happen either in Personal life or Professional life. It indicates a highly emotional time.

(Intuitive, Creative, Scattered)

U is the 21st letter of the English Alphabet. Pythagoras assigned the number 3 (2+1=3) to this letter U. So, U carries all the attributes of the Number 3 as well as the attributes of 2 and 1 to some extent. U comes under the category of an Intuitive Letter. U is an up-shaped letter, which shows its imaginative character and open-mindedness. U has good communication skills. U has many qualities like C, but this letter is much more spiritual than C. U shows a lot of tenacity and does not easily become discouraged. U has a good voice, which helps to excel in music. Negative U is highly emotional, conservative, materialistic, temperamental, nervous, and jealous.

In Future Prediction through Numerology U indicates a financial loss or any old emotional issues that may come again in life.

(Loving, Efficient, Greedy)

V is the 22nd letter of the English Alphabet. 22 is the Master Number. Pythagoras assigned the number 4 (2+2=4) to this letter V. So, V carries all the attributes of the number 4 as well as the number 2. V comes under the category of an Intuitive Letter. If we look at the shape of the letter V, we can see V opens at the top which means the mind is open to the higher philosophy of life. V has the vision, strength, and willpower to achieve any bigger goal in life. V never changes its opinion and has good dealings with others. V is very intellectual and has very good business skills. Negative V is very much greedy, selfish, suspicious, and misuses sexual energy.

In Future Prediction through Numerology V indicates travel and a financially good time.

(Charming, Self-Expressive, Greedy)

W is the 23rd letter of the English Alphabet. Pythagoras assigned the number 5 (2+3=5) to this letter W. So, W carries all the attributes of the number 5, as well as the attributes of 2 and 3 to some extent. W comes under the category of a Physical Letter. If we look at the shape of the letter, we can see two Vs in the letter, which makes W the most balanced letter in English Alphabet. W is reliable, efficient, and adaptable in any situation. W is very much spiritual in nature. W has a lot of interest in occult subjects. W is helpful, practical, and romantic in nature. Negative W is restless, deceitful, irresponsible, liar, and too much sensual in nature.

In Future Prediction through Numerology W indicates travel, change, love affairs, and involvement in legal matters.

(Friendly, Sensual, Unfaithful)

X is the 24th letter of the English Alphabet. Pythagoras assigned the number 6(2+4=6) to this letter X. So, X carries all the attributes of the number 6 as well as the attributes of numbers 2 and 4. X comes under the category of an Emotional Letter. If we look at the shape of the letter, we can find two lines intersecting each other and creating 4 Vs, which makes X very much friendly and open-minded. X has a magnetic personality. X likes to mingle with people and has a great desire to improve mankind. Negative X is revengeful, ill-tempered, unsympathetic, takes advantage of other people for sexual gratification, and suffers from constant turmoil in life.

In Future Prediction through Numerology X indicates some kind of self-pity, love affairs may come or financial gain may happen.

(Compassionate, Practical, Headstrong)

Y is the 25th letter of the English Alphabet. Pythagoras assigned the number 7 (2+5=7) to the letter Y. So, Y carries all the attributes of the number 7 and the attributes of 2, and 5 as well to some extent. Y comes under the category of an Intuitive Letter. If we look at the shape of the letter Y, we can see one vertical line, with two upper forks making a 'V' shape. This 'V' shape indicates its openness to the higher thought at the same time two upper forks create problems in decision making. Y is a deep thinker, with spiritual, and psychic power. Y has musical ability and artistic ability as well. Y prefers silence and the beauty of nature. Y is very much interested in mystic elements of life. Negative Y is restless, sensitive, depressive, talkative, and indecisive.

In Future Prediction through Numerology Y indicates secrecy and minor health problems.

Z

Z is the 26th letter of the English Alphabet. Pythagoras assigned the number 8 (2+6=8) to this letter Z. So, Z carries all the attributes of the number 8 and the attributes of numbers 2,6 as well to some extent. Z comes under the category of Emotional Letter. Z is very much energetic and goal-oriented. 8 is very good at speech and spiritual at heart. Negative Z is deceitful, greedy for money and power, and not comfortable in sharing.

In Future Prediction through Numerology Z indicates a financially good time, and change may happen including residential change.

7

<u>**EXPRESSION NUMBER**</u>

One of the most important numbers in your Numerology Chart is your Expression Number. The Expression Number can be derived from your full name. Much of your talents, abilities, and shortcomings of your character are revealed from your Expression Number. The Expression Number indicates which career you are going to pursue in your life. Your vocation in life is chiefly influenced by your Expression Number. The Expression Number indicates your natural talent. Finding out natural talent is very essential to choose the right career in your life. If your work is based on your natural talent, you can be much more productive and your satisfaction level will be very high. That is why throughout the course of life, the effect of your Expression Number is very high. So, to be more productive and effortless in your career, your Expression Number should be compatible with your birth date number. Your Expression Number indicates what you are destined to become, for this reason, many Numerologists like to call the Expression Number a Destiny Number.

<u>How to Calculate Expression Number -</u>

Pythagorean Number Table-

1	2	3	4	5	6	7	8	9
A	B	C	D	E	F	G	H	I
J	K	L	M	N	O	P	Q	R
S	T	U	V	W	X	Y	Z	

STEP -1

To find out the Expression Number, first, you need to write the full birth-certificate name and write the numbers of each letter based on the above Pythagorean Number Table. If there is any middle name, then consider the middle name as well to calculate the Expression Number.

EXAMPLE:

M A H E N D R A	S I N G H	D H O N I
4 + 1+ 8+5+5+ 4+9+ 1	1+9+5+7+8	4+8+6+5+9

STEP -2

EXAMPLE:

You have to add each name number separately to get the individual total.

M A H E N D R A	S I N G H	D H O N I
4+1+8+ 5+5+ 4+9+1	1+ 9+ 5+ 7+8	4+ 8+ 6+5+ 9
37	30	32

STEP -3

In Numerology, we consider the single-digit number from 1 to 9, except the Master Numbers like 11, and 22 so you need to add the double-digit numbers that you have found in step 2. If in any case, you have found any Master Numbers like 11 or 22, then don't reduce it.

EXAMPLE:

M A H E N D R A	S I N G H	D H O N I
4+ 1+8+5+5+4+9+1	1+9+5+ 7+8	4+ 8+ 6+ 5+9
37	30	32

<u>3+ 7</u>	<u>3+0</u>	<u>3+2</u>
10	3	5
1		

<u>STEP – 4</u>

Now you come to the final step of getting the Expression Number. You have to add the single number that comes from the first name, middle name, and last name to find out the Expression Number between 1 to 9. In any case, if the Expression Number total becomes 11 or 22, don't reduce it because it will be considered as a Master Number. In case the Expression Number total becomes 13, 14, 16, 19, it will be considered as a Karmic Debt Number, which gives certain challenges to us. It is always advised to correct the name under the guidance of an expert Numerologist in case there is Karmic Debt Number found in the Expression Number.

<u>EXAMPLE:</u>

M A H E N D R A	S I N G H	D H O N I
1	3	5

1+3+5= 9

<u>EXPRESSION NUMBER -1</u>

(Determined)

You are a born leader with having independent nature. You are highly ambitious. You are very much confident and enthusiastic about your life and work. You have strong executive abilities. You not only set high goals but also possess the power to achieve them. You have strong willpower. You always love to be at the forefront. Generally, it is believed that 1 expression number people are self-made people, they can leave a mark on their work even after their death. Pride, ego, laziness, and arrogance are some of your shadow sides of the character. Your 'I' consciousness is very high which makes you a self-centred person. You tend to become dominating in nature. You possess a very strong personality, for this sometimes people go away from you and your personal relations get strained.

<u>Suitable Career Options</u> - Arts, politics, law, investment manager, owner, director, head of any organization, writer, musician, computer programmer, actor/actress, film director, army officer, critic, newscaster, broker or money lender.

<u>EXPRESSION NUMBER -2</u>

(Diplomatic)

You get along very nicely with others probably that is your most important talent. So, you work better in a situation where cooperative skill is required. You tend to avoid the limelight. You work well behind the throne. Your musical talent is also very high. You counsel other people very well. Your modesty attracts others. you love to maintain peace in your surroundings that is why you are known as a peace maker. You have strong intuition power. You have all the qualities of being a good diplomat. You are very much sensitive towards your surroundings. You get many benefits from women. You can judge others very well. There are some shadow sides of your character like you become easily hurt if anyone criticizes you, and you are shy and secretive. You do a lot of self-pity. Sometimes you show a careless attitude and become apathetic towards others.

<u>Suitable Career Options</u> - Interior decorator, artist, writer, teacher, psychologist, librarian, diplomat, astronomer, sculptor, civil servant, novelist, dancer, musician, numerologist, astrologer, psychologist, tour director, editor, tarot card reader.

EXPRESSION NUMBER -3

(Happy-go-lucky)

You are a joyful person, who loves to mix with other people. You can express yourself well through writing and speaking. Your creative skill is superb. You are very much friendly to others. Your cheerful attitude towards life inspires others. You are optimistic. You are very much sociable in nature. 3 is a good Expression Number that brings good fortune, provided your Expression Number must be compatible with your birth date number. You are a multi-talented person which is why sometimes you scatter your talent. You should focus on a particular area of your choice to get more success in your life. Time management is very much important for you. You should never misuse your time. Some shadow sides are there in your character. Irresponsible nature, lack of commitment, lack of focus, and lack of confidence are some of them. You do a lot of unnecessary worries which brings sleeplessness. You lose interest very quickly.

Suitable Career Options - Singer, fashion designer, dancer, lawyer, writer, publisher, entertainer, comedian, public speaker, theatre person, performer, singer, jeweller, poet, judge, sales person, landscape artist, restaurant manager, entertainer, food and fashion related any work, model, plastic surgeon.

EXPRESSION NUMBER -4

(Organizer)

You are a very good organizer, realistic, methodical and systematic. You have the ability to turn your dream into reality. You love to make a blueprint of your plan and then work on it. Patience is a great asset of your character. You can make a consistent effort towards your goal. You are conservative. You are good at mathematics. You are very much down to earth. You are very sincere in your relationship. You possess good stamina. You love children a lot and that makes you a good parent. Your money management skill is good. You don't unnecessarily spend money.

You are very good at the technical matter. The shadow side of your character is your feeling of insecurity. Sometimes you prefer to take short cut to achieve your goal. You become frustrated by limitations. You should avoid becoming too much bossy and dogmatic. This Expression Number brings delays, obstacles, limitations, and hard work.

<u>Suitable Career Options</u> - Accountant, lawyer, government official, economist, scientist, architect, dentist, promoter, builder, contractor, author, cashier, doctor, sculptor, military officer, technical writer, gymnast, weight lifter, plumber, electrician, librarian, draftsman, engineer, dean, furniture manufacture, store manager.

<u>EXPRESSION NUMBER -5</u>

(Adaptable)

You are a freedom lover. You can adapt to any type of situation very easily, that is the most positive side of your character. Any type of routine work always makes you bored very easily. You have a charismatic character that attracts others to you like a magnet. You love all sorts of adventure. You love to travel to different places. You are a versatile genius. You have the ability to do anything. Change is the only constant thing in your life. You need to go through different kinds of changes in your life. The shadow side of your character is your sensual nature. You have a very high sex drive, and for this, you may have exciting love life but you need to remember for a healthy relationship commitment is also important. Self-control is very much important for you. You daydream a lot about any given task but lack the consistency to finish it. Self-discipline is another big challenge which is why even if you start any project well but it is not easier for you to finish the project.

<u>Suitable Career Options</u> - Editor, lawyer, politician, travel agent, actor, banker, doctor, lecturer, promoter, flight attendant, photo journalist, automobile engineer, psychologist, sports, stock broker, plastic surgeon, beauty expert.

EXPRESSION NUMBER - 6

(Responsible)

You are a very much honest, loving, caring, and trustworthy person. As 6 is a domestic number, your main focus in life is your family. Your moral character is very high. You are born with artistic talent. You are very kind-hearted and sympathetic to others. Generally, your living room is very beautifully decorated. Guests become very pleased by your hospitality. You are a very good listener, which makes you a very good counsellor. You are a natural healer. That is your greatest talent, people get comfortable in presence of you. You also possess the very good business skill. You are a born teacher. You are a lover of pets. The shadow side of your character is, you become easily tempted to get beautiful things by any means. Different types of temptations may come on your way that you need to fight. You can't trust others easily which sometimes causes a domestic problem. You need constant appreciation, and can't take criticism easily.

Suitable Career Options - Counsellor, designer, social worker, psychologist, doctor, interior decorator, musician, singer, nurse, chef, florist, dancer, poet, media professional, veterinarian, sociologist, costume designer, song writer, cosmetologist, psychiatric, owner of school or hospital.

EXPRESSION NUMBER - 7

(Highly Intuitive)

You have a great analytical and logical mind. You love to explore unknown things. You love to keep yourself away from the hustle and bustle of life. You are a private person. You like to keep your thoughts undisclosed from others. You love to keep yourself busy with the higher thoughts of life. You love meditation. 7 is a number of studies so books are an integral part of your life. You love to spend hours in solitude. You find the answers to questions in silence. It is advisable you can stay alone without being a loner. Your mind loves to engage with the mysteries of life. As your mind is always filled with higher thoughts, so you don't like to deal with mundane activities, with ordinary people you feel cynical. This is the shadow side of your character. You are very much secretive in nature; you can't trust others easily. You need emotional maturity. If your Expression Number is in harmony with your birth date number. It can bring good luck and prosperity.

Suitable Career Options - Research, scholar, philosopher, psychiatrist, psychologist, psychotherapist, astronomer, teacher, inventor, investigator, editor, judge, computer programmer, photographer, doctor, investment broker, astrologer, numerologist, tarot card reader.

EXPRESSION NUMBER -8

(Ambitious)

You are a visionary. You have the power to achieve big things in life. You are very much dynamic in nature. You have great leadership skills. Your money management skill is very good. You can generate a large amount of wealth with your enterprising skill. You love authority and power. Life is not a bed of roses; you have to face sorrow in your life. 8 Expression Number carries a very high karmic effect. You have to face a lot of delays, till you reach your goals. Sometimes delays are unjustifiably long. Your main challenge is to maintain a balance between materialism and spiritualism because the higher loop of 8 signifies spiritualism and the lower loop of 8 signifies materialism. You are not satisfied with any lower position. You have great physical strength which can help you to become an outstanding sportsperson. But above all 8 is a very good business number, and for this, we have seen many athletes settle down in business after finishing their athletic careers.

Suitable Career Options - Sports, politics, musician, composer, environmental activist, writer, editor, publisher, painter, detective, occult expert, travel expert, hair stylist, reporter, surgeon.

EXPRESSION NUMBER -9

(Humanitarian)

You are very much compassionate in nature. You have natural artistic talents. You are a great humanitarian. While 6 represents family love 9 represents universal love. Happiness comes when you do something for the betterment of society. You are a born fighter. You are very much ambitious. This Expression Number makes you busy and hardly gives you time for personal enjoyment. You are romantic as well as daring. You possess a broad view of life; you don't have any prejudice. That is why you have friends from all walks of life. You are a great philanthropic. You have a magnetic personality. You love perfection in the work you do. 9 Expression Number suggests that you are a highly evolved soul. Your life purpose is to enlighten many people through your philosophy. You have also some shadow sides of your character. You are short-tempered, selfish, and self-centred. Sometimes you become very much aloof when nobody can approach you.

Suitable Career Options - Sports, politics, healing, surgeon, spiritual leader, musician, writer, philanthropist, sales person, publisher, defence, doctor, metaphysician, social worker, nurse, lawyer, entertainer.

EXPRESSION NUMBER -11

(Inspirational)

You have come to this world for the betterment of your society. You are a very inspirational character. Your approach towards life is very much idealistic. You are a visionary. You have psychic ability. You can become a great teacher. You are highly intuitive along with it you have all the qualities of Expression Number 2. 11/2 is a highly powerful Expression Number. You are supposed to receive powerful ideas from a higher source. But if you are not aware of your own potential, you get a lot of emotional turmoil in your life. 11/2 is a highly charged number, so you must know how to control your own energy level. You always feel different from the crowd but can't define why you feel so and it creates confusion in your life. That is why you cannot mix well with your age group people. Many 11/2 are daydreamers, as in reality, you don't get the peace you try to take refuge in your dream world. Your main challenge is to be realistic about yourself. It is a number of illuminations so if you have the support of other core numbers in your Numerology Birth Chart you can do great things for the upliftment of humanity. The shadow sides of your character are, you are highly sensitive and too much emotionally vulnerable to your surroundings. Sometimes you become impractical, temperamental, and self-centred.

<u>Suitable Career Options</u> - Artist, musician, actor, spiritual master, occult science expert, writer, teacher.

<u>EXPRESSION NUMBER -22</u>

(Visionary)

You have come to this world to do some bigger tasks. It is the number of a master builder. You have great inner strength and problem-solving skills, and along with it, you have all the qualities of 4 Expression Number. You always dream to create something big. You have an inner desire to leave your mark in some way. You have huge potential inside you to become highly successful. You are not satisfied with your limited achievements. You are a visionary. You are here to serve mankind by successfully undertaking big projects. If you take a service attitude you will be rewarded by a higher power. As you are carrying a highly powerful number so any career field you can choose for yourself. Though 22/4 is a very powerful number still it has some shadow side. If you are not at your higher level of consciousness, unnecessary tension, and worry will grip you. You suffer from a higher level of depression. You become selfish and domineering to achieve your target.

<u>Suitable Career Options</u> - Builder, engineer, architect, director, lawyer, surgeon, writer.

8

SOUL URGE NUMBER

The Soul Urge Number indicates what your heart desires most. The influence of Soul Urge Number can be seen everywhere in your life. Soul Urge Number determines your liking as well as disliking. The soul urge number indicates the passion that you love to do most.

Everyone in this world has a motive. The vowels in your name set the motive to lead your life. It actually tells what you want from your life. Your attitudes towards life are also to some extent governed by your Soul Urge Number.

If your Soul Urge Number gets the support of other core numbers life will be peaceful and balanced. If the soul urge number is incompatible with other core numbers like Life Path Number, Fate Number, Expression Number, and Personality Number tension may arise in your life.

How To Calculate Soul Urge Number -

Pythagorean Number Table

1	2	3	4	5	6	7	8	9
A	B	C	D	E	F	G	H	I
J	K	L	M	N	O	P	Q	R
S	T	U	V	W	X	Y	Z	

STEP- 1

To find out the Soul Urge Number first you need to write the full birth certificate name and write the number of each vowel of your name based on the above Pythagorean Number Table. If there is any middle name, then consider the middle name as well to calculate the Soul Urge Number.

EXAMPLE:

M A H E N D R A	S I N G H	D H O N I
1 5 1	9	6 9

STEP - 2

Add numbers of each part of the name, first name, middle name, and last name to get individual totals. Convert all the double-digit totals to single digits except Master Numbers.

EXAMPLE:

M A H E N D R A	S I N G H	D H O N I
1 5 1	9	6 9
1+5+1	9	6+9
7		15
		1+5
		6

STEP -3

Now finally to get the Soul Urge Number you need to add the single total together and continue adding till you get the single-digit Soul Urge Number between 1to 9. If the Soul Urge Number total comes to 11 or 22 then don't reduce it. It will be considered a Master Number. If the Soul Urge Number total comes to 13, 14, 16, or 19, then the Soul Urge Number total will be considered as a Karmic Number.

EXAMPLE:

M A H E N D R A   S I N G H   D H O N I

7   9   6

7+ 9+ 6 = 22 = 22/4 (Master Number)

SOUL URGE NUMBER – 1

(Independent)

There is a desire in your heart to become independent. Your aim is to become a leader in your field. Any subordinate position does not suit you. You have strong willpower as well as an inner urge to reach your goal. You are very much ambitious. You are able to take decisions confidently. You are very much individualistic in nature. You are a committed person, when you commit to someone with something you always fulfil your commitment. Your willpower is praiseworthy. Your energy level is very high. 1 Soul Urge Number indicates your urge to become successful. You came to this earth to win not to lose the battle. Your inner drive is so strong that helps you to overcome any sort of obstacle. You have a strong passion for creativity. There is an inner desire for fame and recognition. You give importance to self-respect.

The shadow side is your dominating nature. Sometimes you become too much critical and need to be controlled. You are very much impulsive as well as impatient.

In a love relationship many times you demand loyalty from your partner but you cannot express your true feelings. Your serious attitude creates problems in a love relationship. Sometimes you neglect your love life.

SOUL URGE NUMBER – 2

(Friendly)

You always long for a peaceful situation in your life. You are extremely sensitive to your surroundings. Any sad situation makes you extremely emotional. You never want to come to the forefront rather you love to remain behind the throne. You have a great interest in music. You possess a good voice, so you can do well either in singing or recitation.

You can make a career on it. Your real strength lies in generosity, compassion, and understanding. You are a favourite to your friend because of your helping nature.

The shadow side is you cannot finish the project that you start. Lacking a definite purpose in your life sums up to be your biggest challenge. You are not disciplined enough. Sometimes you become pessimistic. Those who have 2 as their Soul Urge Number tell lie very easily.

In a love relation, you are a very good loving partner, reliable and trustworthy.

SOUL URGE NUMBER – 3

(Fun loving)

You love to enjoy your life with family and friends. You are blessed to have a gift of gab. Your talent lies in artistic expression. You are a born entertainer and you love to entertain others with your creative talent. So, it is very important to hone your creative talent like dancing, singing, speaking, writing, and acting. Your soul longs for creative expression, fame, and recognition. You have a very good aesthetic sense. Your solace comes from beautiful surroundings. You have a very good sense of humour. Your cheerful and joyous nature make people happy who are around you. You love to socialize and interact more with the opposite sex. You never bogged down easily in any situation.

The shadow side is you need to be more focused in your life. You must be disciplined enough to use your creative potential, otherwise, you may scatter your energy.

In a love relation, you are very much emotional. You cannot let go of any relationship.

SOUL URGE NUMBER – 4

(Reliable)

You always like to be well disciplined in your life. You love routine. You are very much energetic, so you can accomplish anything. You can never accept sudden changes in your life. You always long for a well-balanced as well as well-organized life. You are a very systematic person and that reflects in all your activities. You are very much concerned about your family. As a parent, you are very good. 4 Soul Urge Number indicates your desire for financial security. You desire to lead your life in a planned manner. Your managerial skill is also praiseworthy. You are a hardworking person.

The shadow side is your rigid nature. That is the main reason behind the rift in your relationship. You need to be more flexible with others. Sometimes you become a workaholic, unable to relax yourself.

In a love relation, you are a reliable partner. You want security. You need a loyal partner.

<u>SOUL URGE NUMBER – 5</u>

(Multi-tasker)

You are a multi-tasker. You can juggle several projects at the same time. You love to travel and adventure. You possess a clear mind to think. You have a natural curiosity for things. You are very much social and love to mix with other people. You feel satisfied when you are free to do anything, no restrictions or limitations are there. You are a very progressive type of person. You are a versatile type of person. Your enthusiasm is very high. Restlessness is very common among Soul Urge Number 5 people. That is why many reporters are having this Soul Urge Number.

The shadow side is your lack of patience. You love the presence of the opposite sex in your life but need to be cautious of over indulgence. You should try to avoid any sort of addiction in your life. You are not disciplined enough. You keep moving from one idea to another idea. You are not very good at doing domestic responsibilities.

In a love relation, your main motive is to enjoy sensual pleasure. You can't stick to one partner for a long time. That is why you may face problems in love relationships. Commitment is very important to maintain a good love relationship.

SOUL URGE NUMBER – 6

(Caring)

You always love and take care of others. 6 is a family vibration, so your main urge is to have a well-balanced family life. You love to beautify your house. You have homesickness. Even if on vacation you love to come back home soon. You are generous in nature. You are easily connected to others as you are a very good listener. You love to extend your helping hands to others. But at the same time, you need to be cautious so that other people may not take advantage of it. You have a sympathetic heart. You are born with natural artistic talent. It will be good for you if you can maintain distance from negative people. You love children very much.

The shadow side is sometimes you become too much emotional. You demand perfection from others, which is not possible all the time and that creates frustration in you. You should not be too much argumentative. Sometimes you unnecessarily interfere in other's personal matters. Criticism frustrates you a lot. You require praise for your instant motivation.

In a matter of love relation, you are a very much loyal and loving partner. You are romantic at heart.

SOUL URGE NUMBER – 7

(Introspective)

You have a hunger for the knowledge you love to think about the mysteries of life. You are an introvert. So, your friend circle is very small. You should practice meditation which is a great relaxation for your inquisitive mind. You have a great liking for occult science. You love to spend time alone. You feel happy when you are left to think alone in your own world without any disturbance. You value your close relationship. You are very much secretive. 7 Soul Urge Number makes you a thinker. You are very conservative in nature. You do not want to waste your time over unworthy issues. Higher education is very much important for you to become an expert in any one field. You have an inner desire for accumulating knowledge.

The shadow side is you can't share your emotions with others, which sometimes makes you a loner. You need to share your real feelings with someone close to your heart. You should avoid being in your dream world always. Sometimes problems arise from your over-analyzing tendency.

In a love relation, you are very much choosy. You keep high expectations from your partner.

SOUL URGE NUMBER – 8

(Power lover)

You long for material comfort. Power and success are the main driving forces of your character. You have a clear vision for your life and work. This can make you a very good business person. You have abundance in your life. You judge things very accurately. You feel happy when you have financial freedom. Life is not so easy for 8 Soul Urge Number person all the time. At every step strength of your soul will be tasted by different types of challenges. You have superb problem-solving skills. You have the power to undertake any big venture. Only the thing that you need to cultivate is courage. The balanced 8 is the most powerful person in this world and your balance comes from the harmonious relation between materialism and spiritualism.

The shadow side is your dominating nature. You must cooperate with others. You should avoid suppressing your feelings.

You are not that romantically inclined to anyone. Love relation hardly matters to you. You want your partner should support you in your venture.

SOUL URGE NUMBER – 9

(Generous)

Your greatest happiness comes when you serve your society. So, we can say community service is the main motivational factor in your life. You are very much intuitive. You are compassionate and friendly in nature. You love perfection in everything you do. Your wisdom makes you a natural teacher. You are very much systematic. You have high ideals. You desire to do philanthropy. You have an altruistic outlook towards life. You are very much sensitive to animal suffering. 9 is an international number so the world is a too small place for you.

The shadow side of your character is your short-temperedness. You should avoid being critical and judgmental. Sometimes you become moody. The only weak point of your personality is your arrogance that you need to overcome.

In a love relationship, you are a very good companion. Remember you are here to serve mankind. You receive more when you give more to others. With the attitude of service, you can get success in your life.

SOUL URGE NUMBER – 11

(The Psychic Master)

You possess clear vision and a clear mind. You came to this world with some sort of psychic abilities. For your inspiring talking and charismatic personality, people would love to float around you. You possess artistic talent. You have strong intuition power. You are an old soul , your wisdom is much beyond your age. You have natural healing power. You desire to make this earth a better place. You should set a worthy goal for yourself and thereby dedicate your life to achieve that. You are in a continuous search for enlightenment. You have an understanding soul as you have had to go through lots of suffering since your childhood days. You have a chance to get fame in your chosen career.

The shadow side is your high-level nervous tension which may lead you to end up your life on drugs and other addictions. You should avoid becoming too much sensitive because it will blur your vision. You need to have a practical approach to convert your dream into reality.

In a love relation, you are romantic as well as idealistic. You are selective when choosing a partner for you.

SOUL URGE NUMBER –22

(Master Architect)

You have strong leadership skills. You are very much energetic. You can contribute to the world in a major way. You have a very high level of awareness. You long to create some everlasting contribution to society. Your inner drive is very strong to achieve any worthy goal. You have the vision to do something good as well as you have the tenacity to continue with your struggle. But your path towards success is not so easy. You are highly ambitious. You need to give yourself time to make your dream into reality. You have all the potential to become a great leader. If you have a grip on reality, you can achieve whatever you want. You are "the master architect" of our society. This is the strongest soul urge number. The shadow side is you need to overcome your doubt and lack of confidence. Sometimes you become very dominating to your family members. You can grow yourself out of challenges. Commitment from your side is very much important to achieve whatever you desire.

In a love relation, you demand that your partner should support you in your mission. So, you need a supportive spouse who can understand your vision.

9

PERSONALITY NUMBER

Soul Urge Number shows the inner aspect of your life, but your Personality Number shows the outer aspect of your life. The Personality Number is an indication of how other people see you. Personality Number comes from the consonants of your full name.

Personality Number indicates all those qualities that you like to project before others.

It is said that the first impression is the last impression. The Personality Number is that impression that you make Infront of others through your behaviour, attitude, and dress sense. If this Personality Number is compatible with other core numbers of your Numerology Birth Chart like Life Path Number, Fate Number, and Expression Number, Soul Urge Number, it gives a positive result, but if it is not compatible then it gives some difficulties.

<u>How To Find Personality Number:-</u>

<u>Pythagorean Number Table</u>

1	2	3	4	5	6	7	8	9
A	B	C	D	E	F	G	H	I
J	K	L	M	N	O	P	Q	R
S	T	U	V	W	X	Y	Z	

STEP- 1

To find out the Personality Number first you need to write the full birth certificate name and write the number of each consonant of your name based on the above Pythagorean Number Table. If there is any middle name, then consider the middle name as well to calculate the Personality Number.

EXAMPLE:

M A H E N D R A	S I N G H	D H O N I
4 8 5 4 9	1 5 7 8	4 8 5

STEP – 2

Add numbers of each part of the name, first name, middle name, and last name to get individual totals. Convert all the double-digit totals to single digits except Master Numbers.

EXAMPLE:

M A H E N D R A	S I N G H	D H O N I
4 8 5 4 9	1 5 7 8	4 8 5
4+ 8+ 5+ 4+ 9	1+ 5+ 7+ 8	4+ 8+ 5
30	21	17
3+0	2+1	1+7
3	3	8

STEP- 3

Now finally to get the Personality Number you need to add the single total together and continue adding till you get the single-digit Personality Number between 1to 9. If the Personality Number total comes to 11 or 22 then don't reduce it. It will be considered a Master Number. If the

Personality Number total comes to 13, 14, 16, or 19, then the Personality Number total will be considered as a Karmic Number.

EXAMPLE:

M A H E N D R A   S I N G H   D H O N I
3   3   8

3+ 3+ 8=14=14/5 (Karmic Number)

PERSONALITY NUMBER - 1

(Dynamic)

You are independent and a go-getter. You are authoritative and dynamic. You are confident and have good self-esteem. You are a very much self-motivated person. You are here to take the lead role. You know the art of delegation very well. You don't like to be ordered but rather love to give order to others. So business is your first choice rather than doing a job. As a 1 Personality Number, you are a pioneer in your field. You look very capable of doing any type of work. You take care of your physical fitness. You like to keep your home neat and clean and well decorated.

Your choice of dress is always neat, stylish, and exclusive. You are very much conscious about your dress. You love to dress in a dignified manner. You should wear a bright colour dress. You always want to see yourself at the top. You take a calculated risk. You can become an excellent entrepreneur.

You should avoid being too egoistic. Sometimes you become very much aggressive, which you should check. Selfishness and pride are your greatest enemies.

PERSONALITY NUMBER - 2

(Gentle)

You are a soft-spoken and friendly nature person. People love your company. You are gentle in behavior. You don't like any sort of arguments. You always prefer harmony in relationship. You have good listening ears that make you more lovable towards your friends and family members. You are very much graceful in nature. You have refined taste. You are the first choice for any type of partnership. As a companion, you are ideal because of your nature. You are emotional as well as sympathetic towards others. You always like to please others. You look very quiet, and friendly with good sex appeal. You are amicable. You can handle the group very nicely. People find comfort in presence of you. Your charming behavior makes you a welcome guest at any party.

You like to wear a comfortable dress. The light colour suits your personality.

You need to guard against your over-sensitiveness. You have lots of trust issues. You cannot trust others easily.

PERSONALITY NUMBER - 3

(Extrovert)

You are a person with a vibrant personality. You possess a charming personality. You are an extrovert. Love to make friends with others. You are very much witty. Because of your joyful attitude, you become the center of attraction at any gathering. You have a great sense of humour. You look very glamourous. You are very much attractive to the opposite sex. Many love affairs may come to your life. But you should commit to a long-term relationship. Your well-groomed and attractive personality may help you to promote yourself in your career. You take care of your appearance.

You like to spend money on dress materials and ornaments. You like to dress up in fancy clothes. You have a good sense of style.

Keeping a promise is a big challenge for you. You lose focus very easily. You need to work hard on discipline. Sometimes you become very much serious. You can't enjoy your life. Sometimes you suffer from mood swings and self-pity.

Personality Number - 4

(Self-reliant)

You project a reliable and trustworthy personality to others. You love to spend time with your family. You are much concerned about money. You don't like to spend unnecessarily. You are a serious type of personality. You love to learn something new. You can't adjust yourself to changes. You are not only devoted to your family but you are devoted to your country as well. You have selective few friends in your life. You are self-reliant in any situation. You do not need anyone to help you. You are a tower of strength for others who want to depend on you. You like the conventional way of lifestyle. You like to be dressed in the traditional manner. Earth colour dresses are very much good for you. While choosing a dress, durability, and quality are your main focus. You are very much impatient and like to do things fast. Your workaholic nature doesn't let you have fun in your life.

PERSONALITY NUMBER - 5

(Fashionable)

You are a very good conversationalist. You are a party person. People feel attracted to you. Your attractive personality and command over speech make you a very good sales person. You are a free soul, don't like any sort of restriction. You are highly energetic. Through your optimistic attitude towards life, you attract others into your life. You are a person of versatile talent. You have a fun-loving personality. Frequent changes of address may happen in your life. This Personality Number helps you travel all over the world. You can be a very good spouse if you get freedom in a relationship. You always like to be dressed as per the trendy fashion. Because of your daring dress style, you are called leaders of fashion.

You need to overcome your Irresponsible nature. You should keep yourself away from any sort of addiction. You need to exercise enough self-control in your life. You also need to control the sensual side of your character.

PERSONALITY NUMBER - 6

(Graceful)

You project a very much caring personality to others. You are very much inspiring among your family and friends. You take great care and responsibility for your family numbers. Sometimes you sacrifice for others. You have a very good artistic sense. You are romantic by nature. People find comfort in your presence. You attract those people who are suffering or in any disadvantageous position. Sometimes you don't priorities your own need as you are busy taking care of others. You are very much affectionate to the children. You are faithful in a relationship.

You have a charismatic personality that never lets you go unnoticed. You love luxury in your life. You are not that much of conscious regarding your dress but you like to dress in a graceful manner. While selecting dress comforts gets priority over fashion. You are not that style conscious, rather you are more concerned about your personality. You are a universal parent you always want to maintain a trust worthy relation with others.

You become easily stressed out. You can't take criticism easily.

PERSONALITY NUMBER - 7

(Enigmatic)

You possess an enigmatic personality. People cannot understand you very easily. People find you a little bit mysterious. You are very much introvert. You cannot mix with others very easily. You only love to talk on the topic that you like most otherwise you love to remain silent. Spirituality dominates a large part of your personality. Higher thoughts of life attract you a lot. You are a very good observer. You have good memory power. Though you look very reserve but you actually possess a friendly personality. You are very much intuitive. You are respected for your wisdom. You like to dress in a dignified manner. A sober colour dress suits you the best. You like to wear quality material.

Sometimes you become very much arrogant. You are very much moody and philosophical.

PERSONALITY NUMBER - 8

(Impressive)

You project a very strong and powerful personality. You possess a very impressive and confident personality. You are very much generous. Your management skill is very good. You have a very active mind. You have good physical stamina. You are good at sports. Your music sense is also very good. You have a chance to shine either in the world of sports or in the world of music. You have a positive and dynamic personality. You are very much selective in making friends. You are sober and reserve. You have the desire to accumulate greater wealth and power. Your enthusiastic personality attracts others. You possess good dress sense.

You never compromise with quality while selecting dresses. Your choice of clothes shows your prosperity.

You should take care of your workaholic nature. Sometimes you become very much greedy for power. You don't like to pay attention to advice.

PERSONALITY NUMBER - 9

(Trustworthy)

You possess a very elegant personality. You are a very kind-hearted person. You are aristocratic. You are very much sympathetic to others. You have a charismatic personality that attracts all. Many people from the creative field have 9 as their personality number. Out of jealousy people may humiliate you. You are a trustworthy person. You have reputation for your punctuality. You have a magnetic personality. You may involve in several relations. 9 Personality Number makes you a romantic lover. You are very health conscious. You like to Stay healthy and fit. You look younger than your actual age. You are a selfless giver. You give whatever you have in terms of time, energy, money, or other resources. Philanthropy is your way of living. It is in giving that actually you receive. Meditation is very much important for you. You like to wear comfortable dresses.

You are very much emotional because of this reason, sometimes you burst into anger. Sometimes 9 Personality Number people have a lot of arrogance in them and that creates problems in their lives.

PERSONALITY NUMBER - 11

(Psychic)

11 is a Master Number in Numerology. 11/2 Personality Number makes you a spiritually conscious person. You mainly spend your life illuminating others through counselling, coaching, and teaching. You have psychic talent. You are very much faithful and loyal. You make friends very easily. You possess artistic talent. You are happy when you are in your world of imagination. You can motivate others very easily. You have a natural power to understand others' minds clearly, which makes you a good counselor. Individuality is seen in your dress sense. Sometimes you like to design your own clothes.

You are very much sensitive, specially to criticism made by other people. Often you suffer from a lack of confidence and low self-esteem. You make enemies without any reason. You don't have a satisfying relationship in your life.

As 11 is the higher vibration of 2, so you have all the personality traits of a 2 Personality Number.

<u>PERSONALITY NUMBER – 22</u>

(Pragmatic)

22 is a Master Number in Numerology .Your personality has the power to make impression on others. Your personality has the power to achieve big things in life. You have a natural talent for handling large-scale projects and accomplishing huge tasks. You are pragmatic and accomplish the task in an unconventional way. You always have a quest to achieve a high degree of material success. You like to dress with the highest quality of clothing but in a conservative style.

You have a very commanding personality. Sometimes you become very ruthless.

As 22 is the higher vibration of 4 so you have all the personality traits of a 4 Personality Number.

10

HIDDEN PASSION NUMBER

Hidden Passion Number is the number that appears the maximum number of times in your name. This number indicates your hidden talent that may or may not be you are aware of. This talent gives you a certain ability that is very much responsible to shape up your destiny. This is the guiding number in your life.

How To Find Out Hidden Passion Number-

Pythagorean Number Table-

1	2	3	4	5	6	7	8	9
A	B	C	D	E	F	G	H	I
J	K	L	M	N	O	P	Q	R
S	T	U	V	W	X	Y	Z	

STEP-1:- To find out the Hidden Passion Number, first you need to write the full birth certificate name and write the numbers of each letter based on the above Pythagorean Number Table. If there is any middle name, then consider the middle name as well to find out the Hidden Passion Number.

EXAMPLE:

M A H E N D R A	S I N G H	D H O N I
4 1 8 5 5 4 9 1	1 9 5 7 8	4 8 6 5 9

STEP-2 :- Now you need to find out which number between 1 to 9 appears maximum number of times in the name. In the above example We can see 5 appears four times in Mahendra Singh Dhoni's name. So, 5 is the Hidden Passion Number.

EXAMPLE :-

M A H E N D R A   S I N G H   D H O N I

   5 5   5   5

Hidden Passion Number 1

You are very much ambitious. You set a large goal in your life and you have the ability to accomplish this goal. You are very much enthusiastic. You have good leadership skills. You can motivate others very easily. You prefer to be your own boss. In career, you are more inclined to business, rather than a job. You can't work well for others. You have creative talent.

Hidden Passion Number 2

You are highly intuitive. You long for a peaceful environment. You are not a leader but you are a very good team member. You work well in a group. You don't like noisy environment. You possess refined taste that can make you a good chef. Your good musical sense can make you an expert in this field.

Hidden Passion Number 3

This number makes you very much social. You love to hang out with your friends and enjoy life. You are highly creative. You can express yourself well through your creativity. You have a charming personality that attracts others. You are a multitalented person. But you require concentration to develop your talent. You are a quick learner. You have good money management skills. As you have good speaking power. You can become a motivational speaker. You need to develop discipline in order to become successful.

Hidden Passion Number 4

You are very disciplined in your approach towards your life. You are very perseverant. You have iron determination for completing any sort of work. You are a very practical-minded person. Your concentration power is very good. You are very much clear in your mind about what is right and what is wrong. You are very much down to earth. You are a nature lover. Sometimes you are very much rigid and don't want to compromise.

Hidden Passion Number 5

You can't stay in one place you love to travel to different places. You have very good command of the language. Your vocabulary power is very strong. You get involved with several things at the same time. So, the focus is very much important to master any skill. You need to maintain discipline in order to become successful. You should try to avoid sensory pleasure and addictions.

Hidden Passion Number 6

You are very much loving. You love to take care of your family. You are very much committed to those you love. People get comfort in keeping in touch with you. You are a very good friend and partner. You always extend your helping hands to those who are in need. Having 6 Hidden Passion Numbers can make you an excellent parent. You are a good listener that is why you are very much lovable. You are extremely negative towards any sort of criticism.

Hidden Passion Number 7

You have a supreme level of intuition power. You are contemplative in nature. You never feel comfortable in a crowd. You love to read books. You have the ability to become an expert in your field. You require faith in your ability to shine in your life. You are very much spiritual at heart. Your concentration level is very high. You are not a people person. You possess a high level of creativity. You don't like to waste your time over unworthy matters. You are a good problem solver. Sometimes loneliness comes that need to be tackled without being a loner.

Hidden Passion Number 8

Materialistic comfort is the main driving force against all the actions you do. You can do well in business. You are a visionary. You have the talent to have great financial success. Especially in real estate, law, and management professions. You should not run after money always. Sometimes you become very forceful which needs to be avoided.

Hidden Passion Number 9

You are very much gorgeous. you have very good musical talent. You are emotional. You are very much enthusiastic. You have artistic talent. You may not be aware of this talent at a young age, but with maturity, this talent may develop. You want to lead an independent life. Sometimes you go into a dream world. The sudden outburst of temper is the negative side of your character.

11

KARMIC LESSON NUMBER

Success depends not only on the strengths of your character all the time. Sometimes success depends on the awareness of the weaknesses of your character and how you can work on those weaknesses efficiently. Your name is the vital source from where you can detect the weaknesses of your character. In Numerology Karmic Lesson Number gives an indication of the weaknesses of your character which you struggle with throughout your life. We come to this world to learn some lessons, which are directly involved with the evolution of our souls. We need to understand first how we should learn this lesson. So, it is very important to understand the Karmic Lesson Numbers with the same importance compared to the other numbers that come from our name.

The letter and corresponding numbers assigned to the letters in your name, give you the power. Similarly, letters and corresponding numbers assigned to letters missing in your name give you the challenges. Now it is your duty to understand these challenges and work on them to become successful in your life. A Karmic Lesson Number is also known as a Missing Number.

Karmic Lesson Number indicates the weak areas of your character. Once it is identified one has to work on those weak areas to get a balanced life. The problems in our life are in many cases linked to those Missing Numbers that's why it is very important to be aware of the effect of karmic lessons in our life. As a parent also if you can understand the Karmic Lesson Number of your child you can give better guidance. So, in a nutshell Karmic Lesson Numbers indicate which quality you should develop in this lifetime.

How To Calculate Karmic Lesson Number-

Pythagorean Number Table-

1	2	3	4	5	6	7	8	9
A	B	C	D	E	F	G	H	I
J	K	L	M	N	O	P	Q	R
S	T	U	V	W	X	Y	Z	

STEP -1:- To find out the Karmic Lesson Number, first you need to write the full birth certificate name and write the numbers of each letter based on the above Pythagorean Number Table. If there is any middle name, then consider the middle name as well to find out the Karmic Lesson Number.

EXAMPLE:

M A H E N D R A	S I N G H	D H O N I
4 1 8 5 5 4 9 1	1 9 5 7 8	4 8 6 5 9

STEP-2:- Now you need to find out which numbers between 1 to 9 are missing in the name. In the above example we can see that 2 and 3 are missing.

1 - A,S

2 -

3 -

4 – D,M

5 – E,N

6 - O

7 - G

8 - H

9 – I,R

Number 2 and 3 are missing from the name Mahendra Singh Dhoni. So 2 and 3 are considered as Karmic Lesson Numbers.

The effect of Karmic Lesson Number is minimized if you have the Karmic Lesson Number in any of the core numbers in your Numerology Birth Chart like Life Path Number, Fate Number, Expression Number, Soul Urge Number and Personality Number.

KARMIC LESSON NUMBER 1

(Lack of Confidence)

You need to be more enterprising. Don't depend on others. Take initiative for your success. Situations always won't be in your favour, so have confidence in your ability. This is the main lesson of this number to become self-dependent. You may face many obstacles but don't be afraid. If you show patience and courage, ultimately you will win. 1 is a number of leadership so you need to develop your leadership skill. You should not become an attention seeker. You need to improve your creative skill. You should not be so much aggressive. 1 is also the number of confidence, so having 1 Karmic Lesson Number in your Numerology Chart means, sometimes you have to suffer from a lack of confidence. It is this lack of confidence that makes you indecisive as well. So don't be shy, learn to promote yourself. You need to overcome procrastination. You need to build courage. You must try to be the best at something. You should not copy, try to maintain your individuality.
If your child has this Karmic Lesson Number then always encourage him to take his own decision. Encourage him to take part in the activity class. The effect of Karmic Lesson Number is minimized if you have the Karmic Lesson Number in any of the core numbers in your Numerology Birth Chart like Life Path Number, Fate Number, Expression Number, Soul Urge Number and Personality Number.

<u>KARMIC LESSON NUMBER 2</u>

(Uncooperative)

2 is a number of cooperation, so if you have 2 Karmic Lesson Number, you may find yourself uncooperative, you need to learn the lesson of cooperation in this lifetime. You need to learn how to become a very good team member. You often find situations where your success depends on how well-balanced your relations are with others. They may be your friends, boss, colleagues, or family members. Adjustment is the key lesson of this Karmic Lesson Number. You need to work on maintaining your emotional balance. Security is the prime focus of your life. You don't like to entangle in any sort of confrontation, sometimes you become very sensitive towards criticism made by others. In order to become successful, you need to be more diplomatic. You need to develop the skill to work in a group. You need to be sensitive enough to what other people need. Patience is required on your part to become successful.

If your child has 2 Karmic Lesson Number help him to learn the art of sharing. This is the most important personality trait; he must develop from childhood.

The effect of Karmic Lesson Number is minimized if you have the Karmic Lesson Number in any of the core numbers in your Numerology Birth Chart like Life Path Number, Fate Number, Expression Number, Soul Urge Number and Personality Number.

<u>KARMIC LESSON NUMBER 3</u>

(Low self-esteem)

3 is a number of expressions, so if you have 3 Karmic Lesson Number that means you find difficulty in expressing your thoughts and emotions. You may feel shy. You need to work on your communication skill. You should try to express yourself more often either verbally or by writing. You should also develop some sort of artistic skill. Try to avoid making sarcastic remarks. You should not be self-critical. You need to be cheerful. You find yourself very much critical. You take life very seriously. That is why you can't enjoy your life. You should try to develop a positive attitude towards life.

If your child has 3 Karmic Lesson Number help him to build self-esteem. Admitting him to a public speaking class or any other group class can be helpful. Encourage your child, and praise him whenever he deserves it.

The effect of Karmic Lesson Number is minimized if you have the Karmic Lesson Number in any of the core numbers in your Numerology Birth Chart like Life Path Number, Fate Number, Expression Number, Soul Urge Number and Personality Number.

KARMIC LESSON NUMBER 4

(Lack of Discipline)

4 is a number of disciplines. So, if you have 4 Karmic Lesson Number means you struggle with methods and disciplines. You can't do your work in an organized manner. You tend to be messy. The key lesson of this Karmic Lesson Number is to learn how to become more organized. Hard work is your companion. You can't take any short cut. Patience is required on your part to achieve any goal. Sometimes you become very judgmental. Surroundings sometimes make you revengeful. You are very much traditional. You need to make a solid foundation if you want to become successful. Sometimes you find challenges in career selection. You should try to avoid being impractical. So often you suffer from lack of concentration. So, you need to develop your concentration power. Sometimes you find the problem in detailing any work, you try to work on a superficial level.

The main problem with your child is tidiness if he has a 4 Karmic Lesson Number. He can't keep his things in the right place. He may be a little bit disorganized with his studies. So as a parent you need to motivate your child how to become disciplined and help him to pay attention to cleanliness.

The effect of Karmic Lesson Number is minimized if you have the Karmic Lesson Number in any of the core numbers in your Numerology Birth Chart like Life Path Number, Fate Number, Expression Number, Soul Urge Number and Personality Number.

KARMIC LESSON NUMBER 5

(Unadaptable)

5 is a number of freedom. So, if you have 5 as your Karmic Lesson Number that makes you always suffer from freedom-related issues. You find yourself in an environment where you are getting restricted. You suffer from the changing situation of life. You can't cope with the changes, that life offers. But change is the only constant thing that our life offers. So, the key lesson of this Karmic Lesson Number is to learn how to adapt to changes. Another problem of this Karmic Lesson Number is the fear of being in any kind of gathering. You don't get confidence in participating in any kind of group gathering. You do things in a hurry. Commitment is very important in your life either in a relationship or in work. You must take care of your health. You need to be a little bit more social. You should not isolate yourself. You should mix with many types of people in society. Your mind is your greatest asset. So, you should develop your mind.

If your child has a 5 Karmic Lesson Number then help your child to be more adaptable to the changing situation of life.

The effect of Karmic Lesson Number is minimized if you have the Karmic Lesson Number in any of the core numbers in your Numerology Birth Chart like Life Path Number, Fate Number, Expression Number, Soul Urge Number and Personality Number.

KARMIC LESSON NUMBER 6

(Lack of commitment)

This Karmic Lesson Number presents you with the situations which give you issues concerned with responsibilities. Too much responsibility gives you a lot of stress. You also encounter problems related to commitment. It creates problems in close relations. So, the key lesson of this Karmic Lesson Number is how to become committed and handle responsibilities properly. You must be kind towards needy people. You must learn to maintain harmonious relations among your family members. Don't entertain pride in your life that may turn into ego.

If your child has a 6 Karmic Lesson Number help them to learn the power of commitment from a very young age. Try to give him small responsibility. Develop a sense of beauty in them. You can admit him to any drawing class.

The effect of Karmic Lesson Number is minimized if you have the Karmic Lesson Number in any of the core numbers in your Numerology Birth Chart like Life Path Number, Fate Number, Expression Number, Soul Urge Number and Personality Number.

.

KARMIC LESSON NUMBER 7

(Skeptic)

7 is a number of spiritualisms. So, if you have 7 as your Karmic Lesson Number that means you are far away from spiritualism. Maybe you are skeptical or dogmatic so it is very important to develop spiritualism in a certain way or become open-minded. The main focus of his Karmic Lesson Number is the development of the mind. With study, it will be easier for you to develop your mind. You should study metaphysical or philosophical books which will develop more awareness.

You need to develop your knowledge, skill, and talent in a specific area. Perfection is the key lesson that you need to learn from this Karmic Lesson Number. It is the perfection in your chosen field that can give you success. So, try to get knowledge as much as possible. It will surely give you material success. Don't chase after materialism blindly.

If your child has 7 as Karmic Lesson Number that means you need to develop faith in your child about his own capability. Try to develop reading habits in your child. He can develop computer skills as well.

The effect of Karmic Lesson Number is minimized if you have the Karmic Lesson Number in any of the core numbers in your Numerology Birth Chart like Life Path Number, Fate Number, Expression Number, Soul Urge Number and Personality Number.

KARMIC LESSON NUMBER 8

(Monetary Blockage)

8 is a number of money. So, 8 Karmic Lesson Number means a lack of financial prosperity. You need to work on your money management skill. This Karmic Lesson Number always gives stress with money matters. You can't hold money. So, the key lesson of this Karmic Lesson Number

is to develop knowledge of how to handle money properly. You must learn detached attachment because you are very much attached to your materialistic world. You should not worry always over money matters. You must be aware of your own limitations. You suffer from health-related issues. You can't control emotions all the time. So, it is very important to bring control over your thoughts, words, and actions. Physical exercise is very much needed for you. Try to take one fruit every day.

If your child has an 8 Karmic Lesson Number, help him to learn how to save pocket money. This will eventually develop money management skills in themselves. Encourage him to develop proper food habits, and help him to avoid junk food. If possible, admit him to any yoga class.

The effect of Karmic Lesson Number is minimized if you have the Karmic Lesson Number in any of the core numbers in your Numerology Birth Chart like Life Path Number, Fate Number, Expression Number, Soul Urge Number and Personality Number.

KARMIC LESSON NUMBER 9

(Intolerant)

9 is a number of universal love, tolerance, and compassion. So, if you have 9 as your Karmic Lesson Number that means you are missing all the above-mentioned qualities in your life. You become judgmental and cruel. So, the first important thing is to develop compassion in your heart for others. This number presents you with the situations which demand your broad-minded attitude. Be more tolerant of others. You must help those people who are in need. Try to engage in community work.

9 is the number of givers. So, if you are parenting a child who has 9 as a Karmic Lesson Number that means help him to learn how to give to others. Take him to an orphanage on any special day. Keep vigilance on the contents, he is watching, it helps him not to become violent.

The effect of Karmic Lesson Number is minimized if you have the Karmic Lesson Number in any of the core numbers in your Numerology Birth Chart like Life Path Number, Fate Number, Expression Number, Soul Urge Number and Personality Number.

<u>CONCLUSION</u>

When there is no Karmic Lesson Number in your Numerology Birth Chart that does not mean there will be no problem but it means you are now aware of your problems and you can handle them well. You should dare to dream big.

12

MEANING OF FIRST LETTER OF YOUR FIRST NAME

Each letter in your name adds a special feature to your character which ultimately shapes your personality. The placement of this letter in your name determines which letter gives you the maximum impact. The first letter of your first name is known as a cornerstone. It indicates how your main character would be. How do you tackle the obstacles of your life. The First letter of your first name is the foundation of your character.

A

(Self-dependent)

You are self-dependent. You are very much ambitious and original. You are a pioneering spirit. You are very much progressive. You are a true leader. You have creative talent within you. You possess strong willpower and determination. The shape of the letter denotes that you want to climb the ladder of success. The shadow side is you may lose interest very soon in any project that you undertake.

B

(Kind-hearted)

Unlike A you don't prefer a leadership role, you are much more comfortable in taking the back seat. You prefer to follow rather than to lead. You are cooperative in nature and like to follow the instructions of others. You are a very kind-hearted person. You have a wide range of friend circles. You can do well in academics. The enclosed shape of the letter B tells that you are a shy and introvert person, and don't want to reveal your inner mind to others. The shadow side is, you suffer from decision-making problems.

<u>C</u>

(Creative)

You are very much creative. Your communication skill is superb. You can verbally express yourself very well. You are very much friendly to others. You enjoy doing social activities. You have the motivation to achieve your goal. You are not always academically well but can apply your knowledge well in your life. You possess a healthy outlook towards life. The shadow side is you are very much anxiety prone and hurt very easily.

<u>D</u>

(Self-disciplined)

You are very much self-disciplined. You have a serious attitude towards life. You are a very conservative type of person. You do your daily activities with much efficiency. You follow any instructions very precisely. As D is also an enclosed letter like B, so you like to keep your thoughts inside you, and don't want to express them to others. Persistence and determination are the best qualities of your character. The shadow side is, you like to remain in your comfort zone and sometimes you become very much rigid.

<u>E</u>

(Adventurous)

You are very much adaptable. You are mentally very much active. You need the freedom to express yourself. You are adventurous. You are helpful to others. You need excitement in your life, often you find the problem in your marital life due to this nature. You have good writing and speaking ability you love to mix with other people. You have lots of enthusiasm. You possess 'I can attitude' towards life. Once you set up your mind to achieve something, you are unstoppable. The shadow side is you are impulsive, aggressive, and restless.

F

(Affectionate)

You are a very affectionate type of person. You can give affection very easily to others, specially to children. You love your home and family. You like to take family responsibilities. You attract situations where adjustment is required. You are very much idealist in nature. You have a good command of the language. You are very much emotional and may withdraw easily when you feel upset. The shadow side is often you suffer from anxiety.

G

(Psychic)

You have lots of willpower. You work best when you remain alone. You are a reserve type of person that is why you are misunderstood by others. Unlike F you are less affectionate to others. You are very much intuitive as well as psychic. You are helpful to others. You should avoid doing anything in a hurry. The shadow side is you lack confidence and suffer from anxiety.

H

(Balanced)

You are a very much balanced type of person. You are extremely aware of the material world. Your executive and leadership abilities are very high. You work well with others. You have a strong mental capability, that helps you to possess money, power, and success. You have a good aesthetic sense. You have strong potential to become successful in life. The shadow side is you always try to please others.

I

(Humanitarian)

You are a true humanitarian. You are very much sympathetic to others. You possess extremely deep feelings. Your heart rules over your head. This creates a fluctuation of mood from happiness to sadness. You show universal love and like to take care of others. You are a very much enthusiastic as well as an energetic person. Sometimes delay makes you impatient. The shadow side is you are very much sensitive, which is the main reason behind the suffering in your life.

<u>J</u>

(Optimistic)

You are a true leader. You are ambitious but do not always show your ambition. You are optimistic. You are very original. Sometimes you feel hesitant to start anything new but once you start you can do really very well. You have good mental faculty. You love changes, usually you become bore very quickly. You love cultural activities. You have a charismatic personality. The shadow side is sometimes you waste your time on unworthy relations and suffer from self-pity for the wrong decisions.

<u>K</u>

(Creative)

You have a high potential for achievement. You can inspire others to succeed. You are very much helpful. You are good at detail work. You are affectionate to others. You have a creative mind. The entertainment industry suits you best. You are very much cooperative. You have a good command of the language, which makes you a very good orator. The shadow side is you are very much moody.

<u>L</u>

(Sociable)

You possess creative abilities but can't show them instantly. You are friendly and sociable. You enjoy social activities. You have fine reasoning abilities. You are very much sensitive. You have originality. You are very much focused on your goal. You have an active life with much movement. The shadow side is you are not very much generous.

<u>M</u>

(Self-disciplined)

You possess the organizational ability. You are serious, hard-working , and self-disciplined. You work steadily, and efficiently to complete any work. You have the strength of character. M is known as the mason alphabet. You never accept defeat easily. Your life is full of radical changes. You love appreciation. The shadow side is, you face constant turmoil in your life.

<u>N</u>

(Imaginative)

You are very much adventurous. You need excitement and variety in your life. You are adaptable and imaginative. You are good at analysis. You are truly a people person. That is why you work well with others. You are a very practical- type of person. The shadow side of your character is you are restless, which impacts your decision-making skill.

<u>O</u>

Service-oriented

You get satisfaction in serving others, especially your family, friends, and community. You are secretive in nature. You have good concentration power. You are straightforward. That is why your friend circle is very much small. The shadow side is often you take on responsibilities more than you can tackle. This creates stress in your life.

<u>P</u>

(Introspective)

You are reserve and very much introspective. You work best when you are alone. Philosophy attracts you the most. You have deep insights into the higher matter. You possess strong psychic power. you must learn to trust it. You have an intellectual mind. You can rise to success on your own merit. You have thirst for knowledge. On the basis of your intellectuality and merit, you are able to make a mark in the field of medicine, science, occult science, law, or similar field. The shadow side is, you usually lack confidence and willpower.

Q

(Goal-oriented)

You have a lot of potentials to become successful but often unused. Your energy level remains very much high and you are capable of superior material achievements like money, power and status. You have good leadership qualities. You have strong willpower, which helps you to achieve desired ends. The shadow side is you are much emotional, and for this reason, your life is on an emotional roller coaster.

R

(Honest)

You are a very much self-determined person. You are honest and like to maintain integrity. Because of this quality in your personality, you are able to rise high on the ladder of success. You have strong willpower. You love to give advice but can't accept others' advice easily. You are a self-starter. You are humanitarian at heart, selfless, and tolerant. The shadow side is, in spite of being an idealist, sometimes you become practical. You are very much emotional, and for this reason, feel upset now and then.

S

(Creative)

You are very much ambitious; you are concerned by impressions made by your achievements. You are very much creative. You are independent and courageous. You are very much friendly to others. You have a tendency to take interest in others' life. You become hurt very easily. You are determined and persistent. The shadow side is you are very much emotional, and due to this character, you can't analyze the situation clearly.

T

(Spiritual)

You don't like to lead, rather you like to follow. You can work well with others but sometimes become anxious. You tend to aspire to spiritualism. You are very much devoted to God. You are actually a seeker and often seek a high level of enlightenment. You do self-sacrifice a lot. You like to follow a routine in your life. The shadow side is you are very much rigid and stubborn. You are also extremely emotional and highly strung.

U

(Artistic)

You have good communication skills. You are very much social. You are very much intuitive. You possess artistic skills but always you may not express your artistic skill. Though you are idealistic by nature you may not attain idealistic ends. Your imaginative power is very high. But that imaginative power if you use in a positive way, it can make you a very creative person but if you use it in a negative way, you might suffer from unnecessary worry. The shadow side is you may scatter your energy.

V

(Master Builder)

You are an inspired leader. You are visionary and have the power to convert ideas into reality. That is why you are called a master builder. You are serious, practical, and self-disciplined. You are very much intelligent and able to think outside of the box. You show great executive power when you set your mind to do anything in particular. Your intuitive awareness is very high. The shadow side is you are very much moody and temperamental.

W

(Adventurous)

Your verbal skill is superb. That is why you are very good at selling. You work extremely well with other people. There are lots of changes in your life. You love adventurous life; stereotype life always brings boredom.

So, you love variety. you have the power to fulfill a great ambition. You are very much determined. The shadow side is you are very much restless in nature, which is why you can't stick to any one point.

X

(Responsible)

You accept many responsibilities, not only for your own life but for others as well. You are always concerned about your home and family. You are very much protective and caring to your family members and to those who are needy. Frequently you become frustrated by life's circumstances. Sometimes you need to see delay. You sacrifice a lot when the situation demands but feel stressed out for this. The shadow side is you suffer from self-pity.

Y

(Seeker)

You are the seeker of life. You love to solve the mystic element. You have a strong inclination to read and research esoteric subjects. You don't like the hustle and bustle of life. You love to stay alone and think deeply. You love your independence. You want to keep yourself separate from the crowd and that makes you a unique person. The shadow side is you often become a loner.

Z

(Dynamic)

You possess extremely dynamic energy. Your self-confidence level is very much high. You have strong willpower that inspires others. You are capable of leadership and can achieve great material achievement. You are a person of firm resolution, even if there are so many obstacles still you remain fixed on your goal. You do not let anything stand in your path to success .with integrity in character you are able to achieve great success in your life. The shadow side is your greed and lack of responsibility.

13

MEANING OF FIRST VOWEL OF YOUR FIRST NAME

First vowel of your first name is the first step towards understanding your personality. It determines how you react to any outer condition. The first vowel of your first name determines your inner self. If the first vowel is the first letter of your name. It's impact is much stronger upon your personality. If the first vowel recurs more than two times in any name, it intensifies the character of that particular vowel. The following interpretation of the first vowel is very much general in nature to understand anyone's personality. So full name analysis is very much important to understand anyone's actual personality.

FIRST VOWEL - A

(Independent)

If A is the first vowel of your first name, you are independent and you have an inquisitive mind, you are highly creative. You perform well when you are in a leadership position. You always strive for a better life. The shadow sides are sometimes you become egoist and cynical. You have a progressive mindset; you don't like criticism. You should keep faith in yourself. You don't like to take any type of order or instruction but you would love to order others.

FIRST VOWEL - E

(Adventurous)

If E is the first vowel of your first name, you have an exciting and eventful life. You are a quick learner. You love to have adventure in your life. You can easily adapt to any situation. You are very much helpful to others. You have a practical mindset. You are very much popular with the opposite sex. You can judge others' character very well. You can become a very good friend to others. The shadow side is you are very inconsistent towards work. You can start any work with good enthusiasm but gradually lack motivation. You are very much impulsive. You exaggerate small issues. You don't like any sort of restrictions in your life. As you are very much quick in your approach, you become impatient with slow people.

FIRST VOWEL - I

(Intuitive)

You are very much intuitive. You take interest in artistic things. You can't settle for the less always, you shoot for the stars. You are very much generous; you are ready to extend your helping hands to those who are needy. You possess humanitarian attitude towards life. You are highly sympathetic and can sacrifice for others. Fame and fortune are there in your life, you get it somehow. The shadow side is when you feel negative you become moody, cynical, and selfish.

FIRST VOWEL - O

(Understanding)

You are a person of great strength, a very understanding and tolerant person. You are a charming, intelligent, true friend, and loving partner. You spread happiness wherever you go, you are very much frank in nature. You have a conservative attitude. Your artistic and creative attitude reflects in your domestic surroundings. Family matters a lot to you. You have a logical mind. You love to counsel others. The shadow side is sometimes you take many responsibilities beyond your capacity and become stressed. You are very much secretive.

FIRST VOWEL - U

(Friendly)

You are a broad-minded person. You are very much friendly. To be a friend or mate of such a person is really a pleasure. You are a lover of beauty. You always focus on the bright side of life. You are able to lift anyone's spirit. Others may have a whole new understanding of their lives if they get a chance to associate with you somehow. The shadow sides are sometimes you are conservative, talkative, indecisive, and scatter your talent.

FIRST VOWEL - Y

(Introspective)

When Y is pronounced as E or I, it is considered as a vowel. It gives similar result of E or I. When Y comes next to a consonant, it is also treated as a vowel, but when it comes next to the vowel it counts as a consonant. When Y is the first vowel of your first name, you become an enigmatic personality, you don't want to reveal anything to anyone. You are very much spiritual at heart. The shadow side of Y is its destructive nature.

14

NAME CHANGE AND ITS IMPACT

Numerology is the science of numbers, where a name plays a significant role to redirect a person's destiny. As per Numerology, every letter in English Alphabet has its own energy,when these letters are combined in our name it produces certain energy. That means through our name we have been carrying certain energy since the day we are born. A slight change in the given name means a change in energy level in our life which can give either a positive impact or a negative impact. Let me clear my point with an easy example. As per our custom when a woman marries, she usually leaves her maiden surname and takes her husband's surname. Now -a -days we have also seen a woman uses both her maiden surname and her husband's surname together. But hardly any woman ever consults a Numerologist to find out whether this new vibration coming from the sudden change of name will bring harmony or catastrophe in her life. That is the reason we have seen many women after their marriages flourish but others don't feel harmony in their marital life, even though the marriage is a love marriage. The equation between the couple may be very good before marriage but it suddenly gets changed after their marriage. Even sometimes problem becomes so intense that it comes to the point of separation. In many cases, we have seen problem comes from the adoption of a new surname. In other cases, we have seen people suddenly for many reasons drop their middle name from their original birth certificate name. Sometimes during board exams also for some technical reason, our name gets misspelled and we have to carry the wrong spelling throughout our life. In all the above cases the impact can be felt either positively or negatively depending upon its relationship with the birth number. If the new name number and birth number are in harmony it gives a better result but unfortunately, if the new name number and the birth number are not in harmony, problems can be felt in our life. Our life gets stuck, and we see unnecessary delays nothing goes right. Sometimes people don't get any positive vibration from the name, given by their parents. There is no feel-good factor in their own name. They don't like their names at all.

In all the above situations name correction that Numerology offers can be a boon to suffering souls. As Numerology is quite popular now- a -days so in this situation many people think about a name change to overcome life's challenges. But except for some special reasons complete name change is not required. Only a name spelling change can do a miracle for the person if he believes in Numerology and follow the guidelines of Numerology with a positive attitude. The expectation of overnight success after the change of name spelling seems to be impractical. It takes a certain time to see the changes. With the passage of time, the vibration of the new name starts impacting life, depending upon the attitude of the person who carries the new name vibration. The result may come in months or it may take years. Here intention plays a great role in how quickly, your subconscious catches the new vibration. With clear intention behind name correction, one can miraculously impact the subconscious mind in a rapid time. Suppose one has to prosper in his career but somehow, he feels stuck in the career for a long time. In this situation if he opts for a Numerology remedy through a name change, he first needs to set a clear intention of improving his career, then only name correction can work on his behalf.

In the acting field, we have seen many actors after changing their names with the help of Numerology got immense success. As a Numerologist, I feel that when a person changes his name vibration, he starts getting a whole lot of new energy which gives him confidence and that is the secret of success. Because when the bad patches start in our life the first thing that we lose our confidence, which is the main reason for our failure. A confident person is never bogged down by life's challenges. Name correction brings visible changes in a person's life which are reflected through his enthusiasm and never say die spirit.

Precautions should be taken before changing the name spelling. Nowadays out of curiosity many people do it themselves just for an experiment, completely unaware of the fact that it can bring adverse effects to their life instead of doing any good. So, the name change should be done under the guidance of an efficient Numerologist. It should not be taken very lightly. Proper knowledge of Numerology is highly required for doing this work. Here by the name change, I want to mean name correction that can be done either by adding or dropping of middle name, changing the spelling of the name, adding an initial, or adding the first letter or first name of either parents or husband. When the above procedures are not working in that case complete name change is recommended. Generally, name changes bring good results in any person's life if it is done correctly.

Here one big question arises whether the name change requires any legal changes or not. People get confused at this point and don't want to go for a name change. You can be rest assured that to get the effect of your name change you don't have to go for a legal change. You can get the benefit of your new name vibration simply by writing the new name spelling a certain number of times as suggested by your Numerologist for a certain period of time. You can even use it unofficially wherever you like. Hope many of your confusions regarding the name change now get resolved. So, a minor change in name spelling can bring smooth sailing in your life.

As a Numerologist, I wish all my readers a happy and prosperous life ahead. Many many thanks for completing this journey of book reading with me. I wish you once again for going ahead in your life confidently with the newly acquired knowledge of the amazing number science called Numerology.

Best of luck!!
"Luck Favours When Number Favours."
Dr. Piyhalli Roy Gupta